DYNAMITE
TELE-SEARCH

Books and CD-ROM by Drs. Ron and Caryl Krannich

The Almanac of International Jobs and Careers
Best Jobs for the 1990s and Into the 21st Century
Change Your Job, Change Your Life
The Complete Guide to International Jobs and Careers
The Complete Guide to Public Employment
The Directory of Federal Jobs and Employers
Discover the Best Jobs for You!
Dynamite Answers to Interview Questions
Dynamite Cover Letters
Dynamite Resumes
Dynamite Salary Negotiations
Dynamite Tele-Search
The Educator's Guide to Alternative Jobs and Careers
Find a Federal Job Fast!
From Air Force Blue to Corporate Gray
From Army Green to Corporate Gray
From Navy Blue to Corporate Gray
High Impact Resumes and Letters
Interview for Success
Job Search Letters That Get Results
Job-Power Source CD-ROM
Jobs and Careers With Nonprofit Organizations
Jobs for People Who Love Computers and the Information Highway
Jobs for People Who Love Health Care and Nursing
Jobs for People Who Love Hotels, Resorts, and Cruise Ships
Jobs for People Who Love to Work From Home
Jobs for People Who Love Travel
Mayors and Managers
Moving Out of Education
Moving Out of Government
The New Network Your Way to Job and Career Success
The Politics of Family Planning Policy
Re-Careering in Turbulent Times
Resumes and Cover Letters for Transitioning Military Personnel
Shopping and Traveling in Exotic Asia
Shopping and Traveling in Exotic Hong Kong
Shopping and Traveling in Exotic India
Shopping and Traveling in Exotic Indonesia
Shopping and Traveling in Exotic Morocco
Shopping and Traveling in Exotic Singapore and Malaysia
Shopping and Traveling in Exotic Thailand
Shopping and Traveling the Exotic Philippines
Shopping in Exciting Australia and Papua New Guinea
Shopping in Exotic Places
Shopping the Exotic South Pacific

DYNAMITE TELE-SEARCH

101 Techniques and Tips for Getting Job Leads and Interviews

Ronald L. Krannich, Ph.D.
Caryl Rae Krannich, Ph.D.

IMPACT PUBLICATIONS
Manassas Park, VA

**DYNAMITE TELE-SEARCH: 101 Techniques
and Tips for Getting Job Leads and Interviews**

Library of Congress Cataloging-in-Publication Data

Krannich, Ronald L.
    Dynamite tele-search: 101 techniques and tips for getting job leads
and interviews / Ronald L. Krannich, Caryl Rae Krannich
        p. cm.
    Includes bibliographical references.
    ISBN 0-942710-90-8: $12.95
    1. Job Hunting. 2. Telephone in job hunting. 3. Social networks.
I. Krannich, Caryl Rae. II. Title.
HF5382.7.K694   1995
850.14–dc20   94-41037
                                                          CIP

For information on distribution or quantity discount rates, call 703/361-7300
or write to: Sales Department, Impact Publications, 9104-N Manassas Drive,
Manassas Park, VA 22111-5211, Tel. 703/361-7300 or Fax 703/335-9486.
Distributed to the trade by National Book Network, 4720 Boston Way, Suite
A, Lanham, MD 20706, Tel. 301/459-8696.

CONTENTS

PREFACE

*W*e're busy people. If we weren't, we wouldn't be in business very long. Busy people have big telephone bills. They use the telephone frequently, because it's more efficient and effective to conduct much of their business over the phone than in face-to-face meetings or through the mail. They talk a lot, send and receive numerous faxes, and log on with their computer modem. They increasingly use E-mail to communicate with clients, colleagues, and strangers.

What are the implications of such behavior for job seekers? You should use the telephone frequently in your job search. Indeed, if you want to quickly build your job search network, uncover job leads, and schedule interviews, you should devote a disproportionate amount of time conducting your job search by telephone.

Few people are effective telephone communicators. Many hate to make cold calls. Some even dislike calling friends and acquaintances. Feeling awkward and uncertain about what to say, they would rather avoid the telephone experience altogether. Many telephone callers use inappropriate openings and closings, have difficulty sustaining a focused conversation, and fail to follow-up important calls.

We wrote this book because telephone communication should be an important component in everyone's job search. Unfortunately, few job search books devote much attention to the nuts-and-bolts of tele-search. When they do, they include little useful information on how to actually conduct a tele-search, promote inappropriate cold calling sales analogies, and fail to include much of the telecommunication revolution that is transforming today's job search landscape.

We approach the subject differently. We start with a very simple, yet sometimes forgotten, premise about hiring—employers hire people they like, regardless of their qualifications. If employers like you over the telephone, they will probably invite you to face-to-face interviews. Therefore, your challenge is to *become more likable over the telephone.* You can do this by observing some very basic principles of telephone communication relevant to the job search.

Beginning with numerous tele-search myths and mistakes, we outline key principles for developing an effective job search. These principles constitute a set of useful tips and techniques for conducting an effective tele-search. They cover everything from conventional telephone conversations and job hotlines to using voice mail, fax machines, and computer modems to communicate with on-line career services. We also include sample tele-search lines and dialogues to demonstrate key principles for tele-search effectiveness.

Within the next few years we expect a tele-search revolution to mushroom around the use of on-line career services. Your telephone key pad will give you increasing access to a whole new world of job search services—from on-line career resources to databases of employers and job listings. Using your computer modem connected to the Internet or to a commercial on-line service, you'll be able to download job information, purchase career resources, view videos, take tests, join discussion groups, communicate with career counselors, network for job leads, transmit resumes and letters, and conduct on-line interviews with employers. Best of all, you can join this revolution now. We expect the telephone may well become your best job search friend.

We wish you well as you dial your way to job search success. If you follow several of our tele-search tips and techniques, you should be able to dramatically increase your job search effectiveness. As you become more likable over the phone, you will turn many of your telephone contacts into interviews and job offers. You may quickly discover that cold calling and telecommunicating are actually fun!

Ron and Caryl Krannich

DYNAMITE TELE-SEARCH

1

WELCOME TO THE TELE-SEARCH REVOLUTION

*L*et's be perfectly clear about what we should and should not be doing when looking for employment. For there are certain unwritten communication rules you must follow if you are to be most effective in finding the right job for you.

At the same time, there are many mistakes you must avoid, mistakes that could possibly turn off otherwise promising job leads and potential employers.

CLEARLY COMMUNICATE YOUR QUALIFICATIONS TO EMPLOYERS

That's what this book is all about—discovering how to best communicate your qualifications to prospective employers who will either invite you to that all-important job interview or offer you the job you really want. Our medium—the telephone—serves as one of the most powerful communication channels for contacting employers, for following up job leads, and for landing jobs. It's a communication medium that is revolutionizing how individuals find jobs as well as how employers identify, interview, and hire qualified candidates. If you want to participate in key job networks that lead to good quality jobs, you must learn to use this medium effectively in the job markets of today and tomorrow.

Finding a job is all about communicating your qualifications to employers in the most efficient and effective manners possible.

GETTING "FIT" IN TODAY'S JOB MARKET

Finding a job is all about communicating your qualifications to employers in the most efficient and effective manners possible. While some employers may already know about your strengths and weaknesses, most do not. For them, you are a stranger who may or may not be worth considering for a position. The employer's goal is to fill a position with an individual who has the best "fit" for the position and organization. Your goal is to find out if this is the right position and employer for you. If it is, you'll need to communicate loud and clear that you are the one who should be hired.

But how do employers get to know whether you indeed are best fit for their position and that you will work well with others in the organization? What it is they want you to do in the process of communicating your qualifications to them? Moreover, what things should you avoid doing when contacting prospective employers— actions that might eliminate you from consideration?

COMMUNICATE POWERFULLY

How do you plan to communicate your qualifications to employers? Will you limit yourself to only surveying vacancy announcements and then responding to them by mailing resumes and cover letters in anticipation that employers will call you for an interview? That's the relatively effortless way to job search success. Perhaps you plan to organize a more proactive job search campaign by uncovering job leads through your personal network of contacts. If so, what role do you see the telephone, fax, and computer modem playing in your job search? Will these electronic mediums help you network, uncover job leads, and get job interviews and offers?

Many job search activities can be accomplished with increased efficiency and effectiveness by using your phone, fax, or computer modem.

This is what the following pages are all about—better communicating your qualifications to potential employers. We'll help you reach some critical decisions on how you can best communicate your qualifications via the telephone and other telecommunications mediums and modes. For we're convinced that many of your job search goals can be readily accomplished at your finger tips through the use of your telephone key pad. Indeed, many job search activities that used to be conducted in face-to-face meetings now can be accomplished with increased efficiency and effectiveness by using your phone, fax, or computer modem. You'll learn how to get employers to take notice of your qualifications without having to spend a great deal of time sending them cover letters and resumes or meeting with them in face-to-face situations.

THE REVOLUTION IS NOW

A communication revolution is affecting the way individuals find employment as well as how employers identify and hire personnel. It's a powerful revolution that is transforming the job search landscape which only a few years ago was primarily defined in terms of a random search for job vacancies through surveys of printed vacancy announcements in newspapers and trade and professional journals or through dependence on employment firms that ostensibly had the "inside track" on job leads and employers.

The revolution is centered around key communication networks which are increasingly accessed and controlled at the level of the individual through the use of telephone key pads and computers. It's a revolution you should not and cannot afford to miss in the 1990s. It will largely redefine the way individuals find employment as well as how employers locate qualified candidates in the 21st century. It's a cost-effective revolution that is destined to increasingly decentralize, coordinate, and better organize job searches for individuals, giving them easy access to employers who wish to quickly fill job vacancies with the best qualified candidates. It will more than cut in half the time spent in finding employment.

WHAT IS THIS REVOLUTION?

The job search revolution is a communication revolution involving the increased use of the telephone key pad for linking qualified candidates to prospective employers. At present this revolution is largely being defined by employers who are responsible for putting into place several database systems consisting of a pool of qualified candidates from which they can draw upon for recruitment purposes.

So far the revolution is primarily confined to a few employers as well as a limited number of individuals who take advantage, through annual dues-paying membership, of the new database systems. Largely centering around the use of electronic resumes, qualified candidates in these database systems can be accessed by employers through the use of search and retrieval software which operates on the basis of "key words." After identifying a pool of qualified candidates, copies of the selected resumes can be transmitted to the employer via computer modem. The employer further screens the candidates in the process of deciding which ones to invite for an interview.

At the same time, these database systems have numerous limitations for both employers and individual job seekers. They confine recruitment and job search activities to a narrowly defined job bank consisting of a pool of electronic resumes which may or may not yield satisfactory results. Much of this revolution is outlined in Joyce Lain Kennedy's *The Electronic Job Search Revolution, The Electronic Resume Revolution,* and *Hook Up, Get Hired*; Peter D. Weddle's *Electronic Resumes for the New Job Market: Resumes That Work for You 24 Hours a Day*; and James Gonyea's *The On-Line Job Search Companion.*

What these relatively centralized database systems miss is a larger and more important decentralized communication revolution centered around the use of the **telephone key pad linked to computers**. Rapidly evolving during the past two years, this revolution literally decentralizes job search communications. It moves control of job information from the hands of employers and database management companies into a relatively open, unstructured, and chaotic information arena of job seekers and employers. This revolution has the potential of taking both job seekers and employers into many more profitable job search and recruitment directions.

Another aspect of this revolution centers on the use of job-related **electronic bulletin boards** found on the Internet system as well as on such popular fee-based telecommunications systems as CompuServe, Prodigy, and America Online. Representing the ultimate marriage of computers and telephone modems in the creation of an electronic job market, these telecommunications systems open a whole new job search and recruitment world for job seekers and employers. Accessing this information highway by telephone modem, job seekers can review vacancy announcements, transmit resumes and letters, and advertise their qualifications nationwide as well as overseas.

The final aspect of this revolution is the increasing use of **job hotlines** assessed by telephone. More and more large businesses and government agencies routinely announce job vacancies via such job hotlines. Typically consisting of a recorded telephone message listing current job vacancies and application procedures, such hotlines have dedicated telephone numbers. Armed with a list of job hotline numbers, job seekers can literally survey thousands of job vacancies nationwide by calling these numbers. For a comprehensive survey of such job hotlines, see Marcia Williams and Sue Cubbage's *The 1995 National Job Hotline Directory* and Career Communication's *Job Hotlines USA*.

Conventional tele-search has undergone numerous changes due to the electronic revolution.

Tele-search is nothing new. It's a conventional job search method widely used by job seekers, job clubs, and employers. For decades individuals have successfully used the telephone for networking, uncovering job leads, and getting job interviews. The telephone has been one of many mediums by which individuals communicate their qualifications to employers.

During the past few years conventional tele-search has undergone numerous changes due to the electronic revolution. Today the telephone is playing an even more critical role in the job search for several reasons:

1. Employers find traditional recruitment methods more expensive and time consuming than using tele-search methods.

2. In the tough job markets of today and tomorrow job seekers need to contact a larger pool of prospective employers in order to connect with just a few employers who will invite them to an interview; the telephone enables them to expand their search considerably.

3. Traditional networking methods, especially face-to-face informational interviews, are increasingly difficult to use in

many job searches because prospective employers are very busy people who have little time to meet with information-gathering and advice-seeking job seekers. More and more employers prefer the efficiency of the telephone. They are more willing to conduct an informational interview over the telephone than schedule a face-to-face informational interview.

4. Many interviews, especially screening interviews, can be best handled over the telephone than in face-to-face settings.

5. The telephone is the key to accessing electronic databases and using electronic bulletin boards—new job search and recruitment mediums that are redefining the way individuals find jobs and employers recruit candidates. The telephone is synonymous with the new electronic job market.

If you are to function well in the job markets of today and tomorrow, you must learn to use the telephone effectively in your job search. This means having the ability to contact employers, follow up job leads, conduct screening interviews, develop networks, and use electronic telecommunication systems and bulletin boards via the telephone, fax, and computer modem. It means developing key communication skills that will be transmitted in both verbal and written forms.

WHERE ARE WE GOING?

The chapters that follow outline how you can most effectively conduct a tele-search via the telephone, fax, and computer modem. We begin by examining the conventional use of the telephone for developing job leads, following up job search contacts, and conducting interviews in the most traditional form—the verbal exchange of information. Here we outline key principles of telephone communications relevant to a job search as well as examine effective telephone dialogues for different stages of a job search.

We also include special chapters on the new tele-search revolution—the role of faxes, computer modems, and job hotlines in a job search. We outline how you can best use these telephone mediums in conducting a powerful job search.

SELECT THE RIGHT RESOURCES

We wish you well in your journey to organize an effective job search that will result in a job best for you. We know at times it can be a confusing, frustrating, and disappointing journey filled with uncertainty and rejections. On the other hand, finding a job can be an exciting journey of self-discovery and self-renewal. You will meet many new people, acquire a great deal of useful information and advice, learn important things about your own values and abilities, and discover some new job and career options you may never have considered before. Much of what you will learn will come via the telephone.

While this book primarily focuses on the role of telephone communications in your job search, you may also want to examine other aspects of the job search and different job and career options. Many of these concerns are outlined in our other books: *Change Your Job Change Your Life, Discover the Best Jobs for You, High Impact Resumes and Letters, Dynamite Resumes, Dynamite Cover Letters, Job Search Letters That Get Results, Interview for Success, Dynamite Answers to Interview Questions, The New Network Your Way to Job and Career Success*, and *Dynamite Salary Negotiations*. We also address particular jobs and career fields in the following books: *The Best Jobs for the 1990s and Into the 21st Century, The Complete Guide to Public Employment, The Directory of Federal Jobs and Employers, Find a Federal Job Fast, The Complete Guide to International Jobs and Careers, The Almanac of International Jobs and Careers, Jobs and Careers With Nonprofit Organizations, Jobs for People Who Love Travel*, and *The Educator's Guide to Alternative Jobs and Careers*. While available in many bookstores and libraries, these and many other job search books also are available directly from Impact Publications. For your convenience, you can order them by completing the order form at the end of this book or by acquiring a copy of the publisher's catalog.

Contact Impact Publications to receive a free copy of the most comprehensive annotated career catalog available today—*"Jobs and Careers for the 1990s."* For the latest edition, write to:

IMPACT PUBLICATIONS
ATTN: Catalog Request
9104-N Manassas Drive
Manassas Park, VA 22111-5211

They will send you, via fourth-class mail (expect four weeks for delivery), one copy upon request; for additional copies, or requests for first-class mailing, send $2.95 per copy. This catalog contains almost every important career and job finding resource available today, including many titles that are difficult if not impossible to find in bookstores and libraries. You will find everything from self-assessment books to books on resume writing, interviewing, government and international jobs, military, women, minorities, students, and entrepreneurs as well as videos, audiocassettes, computer software, and CD-ROM programs. This catalog puts you in touch with the major resources that can assist you with every stage of your job search.

2

TELE-SEARCH STRATEGIES FOR SUCCESS

*T*he telephone is a special type of communication medium requiring specific techniques for effectiveness. Indeed, it's surprising how many people are effective communicators in face-to-face situations but fail to communicate well over the telephone. Lacking face-to-face feedback, they founder when using the telephone to get information or persuade others to take action in their favor. This should not happen to you. Armed with a few useful tele-search techniques, you should be able to quickly use the telephone for conducting an effective job search.

TELEPHONE VS. FACE-TO-FACE COMMUNICATION TECHNIQUES

Communication takes place both verbally and non-verbally in face-to-face situations. In fact, nearly 65 per cent of all face-to-face communication takes place nonverbally. What you wear, how you sit and stand, and what facial expressions, eye contact, and hand gestures you make often communicate more than the verbal content of your message.

Communicating by telephone is another matter altogether. Telephone communication has fewer nonverbal components. What you say, how you say it, and the sound and tone of your voice become major elements in communicating a telephone message. Consequently, someone who is an effective face-to-face communicator—one who is especially good in communicating nonverbal messages—may be a less effective telephone communicator. On the other hand, many people are very effective telephone communicators but do less well in face-to-face situations where nonverbal communication plays a key role.

One of the major reasons individuals are reluctant to use the telephone is because telephone communication lacks the visual nonverbal components. Having to focus primarily on the verbal component of their message—what to say and how to say it—many people feel uncomfortable on the telephone; they do not feel in control of the communication situation. This is especially true if they must make cold calls and talk to strangers, especially if those strangers have the power to make hiring decisions.

How well do you communicate over the telephone? Do you think you communicate better in face-to-face situations? Do you enjoy using the telephone, even when making cold calls and talking to strangers about employment questions? We'll examine these questions and issues by focusing on commonly held myths and start the process of developing effective tele-search communication strategies.

MYTHS AND REALITIES

MYTH 1: **Face-to-face communication is more effective than telephone communication.**

REALITY: This may be true in many situations, but not necessarily so in all situations. Face-to-face communication is most effective in a formal job interview where both interviewer and interviewee need to communicate critical information both verbally and nonverbally. Such encounters enable them to assess eyeball-to-eyeball whether or not they will "like" working with each other.

There are appropriate times and places for both telephone and face-to-face communication. You need to know the difference.

Telephone communication is most effective for quickly acquiring information and developing job leads, conducting screening interviews, and following-up specific job search activities. Even many informational interviews are best conducted over the phone rather than in face-to-face settings. In a job search it's important to know when to use the telephone versus when to meet someone in person. If not, you may waste a great deal of time—both your's and others'—trying to set up face-to-face meetings when a telephone call would be more appropriate. In other words, there are appropriate times and places for both telephone and face-to-face communication. Know the difference before contacting someone for a meeting.

MYTH 2:   **It is always preferable to schedule a face-to-face meeting with a prospective employer than to conduct business over the telephone.**

REALITY: Too many job seekers automatically assume that all job search communication should take place in face-to-face settings. They mistakenly spend a great deal of time on the telephone trying to schedule face-to-face meetings rather than acquire useful job search information. Being persistent, they pester people for appointments, arrange time-consuming meetings that have no useful outcomes or benefits, and then wonder why so many people wish to avoid or reject them!

Always assume prospective employers are very busy people with little or no time to see you.

Always assume prospective employers are very busy people with little or no time to see you. Further assume that time is money—their meeting time with you is worth at least $200 an hour. Are you giving them a $200 an hour benefit or are you simply exploiting them by taking $200 from their pockets? If they are not busy and don't mind being exploited, they are probably not worth talking to for information, advice, and referrals! Based on these "busy person" and "$200 an hour" assumptions, you need to decide whether it's really important to meet in person or conduct your business over the telephone. To force yourself on a very busy person may have negative consequences for you and your candidacy: the prospective employer sees you as a very aggressive, annoying, and exploitative individual who is used to getting his or her way. Always ask yourself this question before scheduling a face-to-face meeting: *"Is this meeting really necessary or can my business be better handled over the telephone?"* You'll be amazed how often the answer to this question results in an effective telephone call. Make it a practice to only schedule face-to-face meetings when they are absolutely necessary. Keep those meetings to an minimum—only at critical points and with key individuals in your job search.

Good face-to-face communication must be supplemented with excellent telephone, fax, and telecommunication skills.

MYTH 3:   **Face-to-face communication is less important than telephone, fax, and telecommunication skills.**

Interpersonal, face-to-face communication is still very important. The old sales adage that *"Just showing up"* contributes to at least fifty percent of a sale is applicable to a job search—at some point, both before and during the job interview, you simply must show up and demonstrate your interpersonal skills and degree of likability! However, good face-to-face communication must be supplemented with excellent telephone, fax, and telecommunication skills. Interpersonal, face-to-face communication is not enough in today's job search world. You must become proficient in several communication mediums.

MYTH 4:   **Cold calling techniques are inappropriate to use for finding a job.**

REALITY: Cold calling techniques get mixed reviews in a job search. Many people use them with success—especially job clubs which are organized for uncovering job leads and acquiring useful job information and referrals via cold calling techniques. Many individuals have also been successful in using such techniques. However, the problem with cold calling is that it is a **probability method**. Only one in fifty cold calls, for example, may result in useful information or a promising job lead. In other words, cold calling techniques do work, but their effectiveness rate is very low compared to other job search approaches. To be most effective, you must make dozens, perhaps hundreds, of cold calls of which 98 percent will probably result in rejections or no useful referrals. But the two percent success rate, as well as the information-rich experience in talking with many strangers who may volunteer useful information, is probably well worth the effort. Our recommendation: include cold calling techniques in your repertoire of job search approaches, but do not have high expectations of effectiveness nor be disappointed with the large number of rejections resulting from this low probability approach. If you plan to conduct cold calls, make sure you develop a cold calling approach that results in better than average results.

MYTH 5: **You should always have a person's name before making a cold call.**

REALITY: Ideally it's always preferable to have the name of a person to address your call to. However, it's not always possible to know the name of the right person you need to talk to for job information, advice, referrals, and leads. When this happens, you need to do some research to get the name of the right person. You can easily do this by calling ahead and asking a receptionist for this information. The call might go something like this:

> *"Hi, this is Mary Simonsen. I need information about your in-house training. Who is in charge of that department? Does that department have a direct phone number?"*

A question framed in this manner should result in the name and phone number of the person you need to talk with.

MYTH 6:   **The purpose of a tele-search call should be to schedule an interview with an employer.**

Tele-search calls have several purposes. These include getting job information, advice, and referrals and perhaps scheduling an informational or job interview. Individuals are more likely to talk with you if you are only calling for information, advice, and referrals. Expect to get resistance in scheduling informational interviews. A job interview is something you get invited to—it should not be the purpose of a tele-search call.

MYTH 7:   **You should be honest when introducing yourself over the telephone—you are looking for a job and hope the person can help you find one.**

You should always be honest. But there is a difference between being honest and being stupid. Too many people confuse the two and thus say inappropriate things that turn off listeners. Confessing your need for a job and then asking someone over the phone for a job borders on stupidity—you're a stray dog seeking shelter. Such honesty and frankness is not appreciated by most people. You put them on the spot by making them feel responsible for your employment fate. They neither need nor want such a burden. Their initial reaction to your frankness will be to get rid of you as quickly as possible—here's a job seeker who wants me to give them a job! You want to be honest and smart. While you are looking for a job, you should not blurt out that fact to everyone you encounter. Your approach should be honest and tactful. Inform your listener that you are in the process of making a job change; you would value any information, advice, or referrals they might be able to share with you. You might lessen their reluctance to become involved in your employment situation by stressing from the very beginning that you are not looking for a job through them—only seeking information, advice, and referrals. This approach usually results in cooperation. They now become advisors. Most people love to give advice! But they hate being put in a position of being responsible for someone's employment fate.

MYTH 8: **You must be aggressive when using the telephone in a job search.**

REALITY: Except for those seeking sales positions requiring cold-calling skills, aggressive personalities are seldom appreciated by employers. Aggressive job seekers are often obnoxious and threatening individuals. They exude a "take charge" attitude that potentially threatens others in the workplace. Employers appreciate bright, enthusiastic, positive, and likable individuals who clearly communicate their value and appear to "fit into" the organizational culture. Develop non-aggressive tele-search techniques that communicate your enthusiasm, likability, and value to employers.

MYTH 9: **A tele-search call should last no more than three minutes.**

REALITY: A tele-search call can last thirty or more minutes—perhaps even an hour! It depends on the person, the situation, and your questioning techniques. If you are scheduling a meeting, the call may only take a minute or two. However, if you are calling for information, advice, and referrals—in other words, conducting an informational interview over the telephone—the call could take twenty minutes or more. Many people who are asked for information and advice over the telephone tend to spend more time doing so than initially expected. In fact, you may have difficulty getting them to close the conversation!

MYTH 10:   **An informational interview should always be conducted in a face-to-face setting and take approximately 30 minutes.**

REALITY: The telephone should become your most important medium for developing, managing, and following-up your job search communications. Many of your best informational interviews will probably take place over the telephone. In fact, you should plan to conduct at least 95 percent of your informational interviews by telephone; the remaining 5 percent should be reserved for individuals that you simply must see in person. You will quickly find telephone informational interviews to be one of your major avenues for making job search progress. Telephone informational interviews are more efficient than face-to-face informational interviews. For every face-to-face informational interview you conduct, you could conduct at least ten telephone informational interviews. While the quality of information, advice, and referrals gained in face-to-face informational interviews may be superior to that gained in telephone informational interviews, the difference may be marginal at best, if at all. Our advice: limit the number of face-to-face informational interviews to a critical mass of individuals who are essential to your job search. Always ask yourself this question before placing a telephone call for scheduling a face-to-face informational interview: *"Is this meeting really necessary or would the interview be better conducted over the phone?"*

MYTH 11:   **Informational interviews and networking are highly overrated. Most employers do not want to be pestered by information-seeking job seekers.**

REALITY: There is nothing wrong with the informational interview and networking—only methods used by those who engage in such activities. Let's be honest: the informational interview is one of the most misunderstood and abused job search techniques practiced by people who should know better. Many people use the informational interview to get jobs. Not knowing how to properly conduct such an interview, they abuse their invitations, make pests of themselves, and waste peoples' time. Scheduling such interviews for the ostensible purposes of acquiring useful information, advice, and referrals, they then proceed to put people on the spot by asking them for a job. Remember, people who count the most are usually busy people. Many of these people prefer avoiding networkers who use the informational interview to ask for a job. Most people who have been the object of informational interviews also know such interviews can be easily conducted over the telephone rather than in face-to-face meetings which are so time consuming. If you find people unwilling to meet with you for an informational interview, chances are it's not because informational interviews and networking don't work. Rather, it may be your approach. Most people are quite rational—they see no benefit in meeting with you; some fear you will become their burden, you may try to exploit them, or you will waste their time. You'll need to overcome many of these unspoken objections to meeting with you. The easiest way to do this is to conduct an informational interview over the phone. This is relatively nonthreatening and usually takes less time than a face-to-face meeting.

MYTH 12: **You should avoid leaving messages on voice mail; keep calling until you reach a real person or send a letter.**

REALITY: If you keep calling, you are likely to get nowhere. Today's voice mail systems are a real problem for job seekers who increasingly have difficulty getting through to their targeted party. If you call early in the morning or very late in the day you may get directly through to the individual who may have the voice mail turned off. But it's best to assume, before you call, that you are likely to encounter a voice mail system which asks you to leave a message. Therefore, you should first have the name of a person you wish to speak with. Second, always leave a message if you are asked to do so. Third, if you leave messages three times and your calls are not returned, call again and speak with the operator. Ask the operator when the person might be in since you have not been successful in getting through to them. But it's most important for you to know what to say when leaving a voice mail message. In fact, few people know how to leave messages that result in returned phone calls; many rudely hang up or leave very limited information. When asked to leave a message, do not just leave your name and phone number. Busy people who review their voice mail messages prioritize which calls they will return; few people return all of their calls. A name and phone number from a stranger means nothing and to many busy people does not deserve a return call. You must leave a message that will motivate the individual to return your call. The best type of message will be a referral message:

> *"Hi, this is Mary Simonsen at 819-331-4787. John Wilkinson at R.C. Stone Company recommended that I give you a call. It's now 1:45pm and I'll be in the rest of the day. John said I should talk to you about your direct-sales work."*

This message connects you with the individual through a referral—John Wilkinson. You let the person know when you are available and the general nature of your conversation. The point is to not leave too little or too much information—just enough so that the individual will be sufficiently motivated to return your call. If you make a cold call without the benefit of a referral, again, leave enough information. The message might be something like this:

"Hi, this is Mary Simonsen at 819-331-4787. It's now 1:45pm and I'll be in the rest of the day. I would like to talk to you about some of the wonderful work you have been doing in direct-sales."

While the individual does not know why you are calling, he should return your call. After all, you may have a benefit to offer him. Perhaps you are a potential customer, a reporter who will publicize his work, or maybe an admirer who has information to share with him. This message leaves just enough information to motivate someone to return your cold call.

MYTH 13: **You should always follow-up a tele-search call with a handwritten thank you letter.**

You may need to follow-up with another follow-up call. Handwritten thank you letters are not necessary—they appear too personal and this is business correspondence. Demonstrate your professionalism with a nicely typed business letter expressing your gratitude. This is a thoughtful thing to do—and thoughtful people tend to be remembered the most in a job search.

MYTH 14: **Never fax a resume or job search letter.**

It's okay if requested to do so by a job search contact or employer. However, do not send an unsolicited resume by fax—this is a "junk fax" that borders on violating federal laws against unsolicited fax advertising. When requested to fax a copy of your resume and/or letter, be sure to immediately follow-up with a hard copy of the requested communication. Put a note on the hard copy stating it was faxed on a particular date—"Faxed 7/9/95." By sending a copy of the original by mail, you will remind the recipient about your interests and qualifications.

MYTH 15:   **Electronic resumes are the wave of the future. You must have one in order to get a good job.**

Electronic resumes are one of several types of resumes that are proliferating on today's new information highway. While over 90 percent of all resumes received by employers are conventional paper resumes, new electronic resumes are increasingly important for job seekers and employers alike. More and more employers use the latest resume scanning technology to quickly screen hundreds of resumes. Therefore, it also may be in your interest to write a "computer friendly" resume based on the principles of electronic resumes. These principles, along with examples, are outlined in two new books on this subject—Peter D. Weddle, *Electronic Resumes for the New Job Market: Resumes That Work for You 24 Hours a Day* (Impact Publications, 1995) and Joyce Lain Kennedy, *Electronic Resume Revolution* (Wiley, 1994). These are very different resumes compared to conventional resumes. Structured around "keywords" or nouns which stress capabilities, electronic resumes may be excellent candidates for resume scanners but weak documents for human readers. Keep in mind that electronic resumes are primarily written for electronic scanners and high-tech distribution systems (job banks) rather than for human beings. Since human beings interview and hire, you should first create a high impact resume that follows the principles of human communication and intelligence. We also recommend developing a separate electronic resume designed for electronic scanners. At the same time, conventional and electronic resumes are not the only types of resumes being produced today. Some individuals now produce live action **video resumes**. Somewhat of a misnomer, video resumes are more on-screen interviews or summaries of qualifications rather than actual resumes. New electronic technology also has given rise to the **multimedia resume** which blends sound, graphics, animation, and text. Indeed, software is now available (Macromedia's *Director* and *Action!* and Apple's *HyperCard*) which enables you to produce the ultimate multimedia resume—a real plus for anyone in the field of graphics and design. Also, several online services, such as America Online and CompuServe and Internet's Online Career Center, permit users to submit multimedia resumes via electronic mail (for Internet's Online Career Center, E-mail your request to occ-info@occ.com or call 317-293-6499). What is common to many of these new types of resumes is that they can be transmitted via fax or a modem.

MYTH 16: **Individuals who join resume banks are more likely to get high paying jobs than those that don't.**

Electronic resume banks, such as Job Bank USA, SkillSearch, and University Pronet, offer alternative ways of distributing resumes to employers. Essentially a high-tech approach to broadcasting resumes, membership in one of these groups means your resume literally works 24 hours a day. Major employers increasingly use these resume banks for locating qualified candidates, especially for screening individuals with technical skills. And we know some individuals who join these resume banks do get jobs. However, not everyone belonging to these groups get interviews or jobs because of such membership. Nor is there evidence that membership results in higher paying jobs than nonmembership. The real advantage of such groups is this: they open new channels for contacting employers with whom you might not otherwise come into contact. Indeed, some employers only use these resume banks for locating certain types of candidates rather than use more traditional channels, such as newspapers and employment offices, for advertising positions and recruiting candidates. Therefore, it might be wise for you to join one of these groups. They could well open up new job leads you would not otherwise uncover.

MYTH 17:   **Telecommunication systems such as CompuServe, Prodigy, and America Online, with access to the Internet, are a great new way to find quality jobs.**

This job search method gets very mixed reviews. It's a new and relatively uncharted frontier run by a lot of high-tech cowboys and technicians who know little about the content of specialty communications, especially the art of job finding. There's a lot of hype and hoopla about conducting an electronic job search as well as using such information-saturated telecommunication systems. It's still uncertain whether many of these telecommunication systems are more information distractions and time-killers than truly useful and usable databases for most individuals, and especially for job seekers. Many of these systems approximate a game of chance, with slim odds of getting really useful information. Nonetheless, you may get lucky by trying your hand at venturing into this uncertain frontier. At present this job search channel is relatively unstructured, chaotic, and loaded with useless noise, questionable "authorities", and few quality job listings and employers. It's uncertain if many people get jobs by using this new technology and the so-called "information highway." Many advertised jobs on electronic bulletin boards are probably hard-to-fill positions—similar to positions found in classified job ads—or for individuals with high-tech skills. The most useful outcome of this telecommunication channel may be to get information and advice from individuals who are knowledgeable about your particular job field and interests. Information found in many job search books, usually in the form of excerpts, is now available through many of these services. Indeed, excerpts from several of our own books can be found on E-Span Job Search (800-682-2901), a free service on the Internet or through CompuServe, which includes nearly 150 employers and 3,500 job seekers who submit resumes through E-mail. But the quality and quantity of such information is unpredictable and short-lived. It depends on whom you encounter at any particular moment. But be careful. Do not become obsessed with this technology to the point where you spend a disproportionate amount of your job search time trying to telecommunicate for jobs. Use your phone and computer modem to plug into this information highway, but keep it in proper perspective. Our advice: don't spend more than 15 percent of your job search time on the computer. This new technology tends to disproportionately appeal to high-tech candidates and to individuals, especially men, who have a simplistic view of how to get a job—a quick and easy method at the tip of their fingers or with the lick of a postage stamp. The job search is much more complicated and requires a great deal of telephone, mail, and face-to-face work. In the meantime, it doesn't hurt to explore emerging opportunities on the new information highway, such as those found on Internet's Online Career Center, for job leads and vacancy announcements. We expect it will take at least five years before the electronic job search becomes a useful reality. And we expect services on the Internet will become the main players rather than America Online, CompuServe, or Prodigy which we see as transitional systems. Keep an eye on a newly formed service called CareerWeb which will be available on the Internet beginning in May 1995. CareerWeb is likely to become a long-term player in this highly competitive online career business. In the meantime, three useful books on this subject are Joyce Lain Kennedy's *Electronic Job Search Revolution* and *Hook Up, Get Hired* (Wiley) and James Gonyea's *The On-Line Job Search Companion* (McGraw-Hill).

35 DEADLY TELE-SEARCH MISTAKES

Many people are awkward telephone communicators. They don't know how to effectively open and close telephone calls, acquire useful information, nor get remembered for future reference. They make several mistakes that turn off the very people they hope to develop a rewarding relationship with. In a job search, such awkwardness can be deadly.

Some of the most common tele-search pitfalls and mistakes we have encountered include the following:

1. **Use of the telephone inappropriately:** You should never use the telephone or fax when you should be sending a letter. Some of the most effective job search communication, such as resumes and thank you letters, should be done through the mail. You should maximize the impact of your communication by only using the telephone and fax when necessary.

2. **Memorize or read prepared telephone scripts:** The quickest way to turn off someone over the telephone is to waste their time with a script that is memorized or read word for word. You'll sound rehearsed and dishonest.

3. **Neglect to conduct a proper telephone follow-up campaign:** Follow-up, follow-up, follow-up! Many job seekers are ineffective because they fail to follow-up. And many fail to follow-up because they don't know how to use the telephone. The telephone remains the single most important medium for conducting effective follow-ups of written communication. If, for example, you send a resume and cover letter in response to a classified ad or vacancy announcement, don't expect a reply unless you make a follow-up telephone call. Your cover letter should conclude with a statement of action—that you will call within the next ten days to inquire about the status of your application. And be sure to make that telephone call. Also, as you close a job interview, be sure to close with an action statement. Ask the interviewer when he or she plans to make a final decision. Then ask if it would be okay for you to call them the week after their decision date, if you have not heard from them. And, again, be sure to make this critical follow-up call. Each time you make a follow-up call you communicate to the prospective employer that you are still interested in the position. You emphasize the fact that you are a

purposeful and thoughtful individual. This telephone call may well be the single most important action you take to separate you from the competition. Most important, it keeps your name in their minds.

4. **Schedule face-to-face informational interviews rather than conduct telephone interviews:** Many job seekers schedule unnecessary face-to-face meetings that waste the time of both themselves and their targeted subjects. Most informational interviews can be conducted over the telephone. You'll find the quality of information, advice, and referrals you receive over the telephone will probably be just as good as those received in face-to-face meetings. Better still, you can conduct ten times as many informational interviews over the telephone than in face-to-face settings. Don't waste your time nor the time of others with unnecessary meetings. The telephone should become your most important medium for gathering information, developing networks, uncovering job leads, and following-up applications and interviews. Failure to develop an effective tele-search strategy will result in a weak job search. You simply must use the telephone often and at critical times in your job search in order to be most effective in today's job market.

5. **Fail to follow-through the follow-up:** If you say you will follow-up, you must follow-up. And if you follow-up and get little or no response, you need to follow-up again and again and again, until you move an issue to a decision point. If, for example, you follow-up your application (resume and cover letter) with a phone call and are told *"no decision has been made yet,"* ask when a decision might be forthcoming. Then call again within a week from that decision date. Keep calling until you get some resolution, which may be positive or negative. Your calls, especially the fourth or fifth one, will get the attention of the employer who will probably take a second or third look at such a persistent candidate to eventually give you a definitive answer. If the answer is negative, that's okay. If you have been persistent rather than a pest, the decision probably would have been negative without your phone calls. At least you moved this issue to

a decision point. You can now concentrate your follow-up efforts on other employers. The same scenario relates to the job interview. Keep following up until you receive a *"yes"* or *"no"* decision. In the process, you may get a *"yes"*!

6. **Too quickly hang up without sustaining an informative conversation:** Many tele-searchers fail to conduct an informative conversation that results in useful information or action. You should plan exactly what you want to say, from the very introduction to the closing. Between the two ends, you need to ask specific questions. Write your questions down so you don't forget to ask them.

7. **Avoid making cold calls:** Most people dislike making cold calls. Similar to initiating a conversation with a stranger, they would rather write a letter than pick up the phone to dial someone they do not already know from previous meetings or conversations. This reluctance to introduce oneself to strangers can be overcome by learning a few cold calling techniques. Indeed, some people learn such techniques so well that they actually look forward to making several cold calls each day. They enjoy talking with strangers in the process of acquiring information and developing new relationships.

8. **Call the wrong person:** Make sure you are calling the right person. And the right person in most cases is the person who has the power to hire. This person probably is not found in the personnel department. Do your research before you make your phone call.

9. **Fail to keep good records of tele-search calls:** You should always keep good records of your job search communications for follow-up purposes as well as refer to notes of previous conversations when speaking with prospective employers. You'll experience embarrassing moments if you confuse your callers!

10. **Use vocalized pauses, negative terms, and poor diction and grammar.** Many people fail to communicate compe-

tently. Using vocalized pauses, such as *"ahs"* and *"uhms"* to fill silence, they distract the listener from their message. Worst of all, such vocalized pauses are annoying. They use ambiguous and somewhat negative terms such as *"pretty good"* or *"fairly well"*—terms that say little if anything. Even many so-called educated people do not use good grammar. Many people also use poor diction by shortening words. For example, many people say *"goin"* instead of *"going,"* or *"gonna"* rather than *"going to."* Another diction problem is substituting, eliminating, or adding consonants: *"Adlanta"* rather than *"Atlanta,"* *"din't"* rather than *"didn't,"* *"idear"* rather than *"idea."* Do you ever say *"yea"* rather than *"yes"*? The use of sloppy speech is a habit many people—including the well educated—get into. But it is a habit you can change. If you have a tendency to modify words in any of these ways, it is a habit worth correcting.

11. **Use verbs that are not action oriented:** Many people still use the passive voice when talking about what they do. When talking about what you have done or will do, use action verbs like *"organized,"* *"analyzed,"* or *"supervised"* rather than the nouns *"organizer,"* *"analyst,"* or *"supervisor."* When talking about your present strengths, use even stronger action words: *"organize,"* *"analyze,"* and *"supervise."* Always avoid the passive voice. Instead of saying *"The entire conference was organized by me"* (passive), say *"I organized the entire conference"* (active).

12. **Run out of things to say.** It's both embarrassing and awkward to initiate a telephone conversation and then run out of things to say. Be sure to plan—from opening to closing—the content of your telephone communication. List a set of questions you need to ask and refer to them during your conversation. Make notes but **do not** memorize or write out everything and read it! Keep the conversation interesting and moving, from beginning to end.

13. **Fail to ask informative questions or ask the wrong questions altogether.** The quality of your questions reflects on your intelligence and the quality of your candidacy.

Avoid asking simple *"yes"* or *"no"* questions. Focus on open-ended questions that require the other person to provide useful information. For example, instead of asking *"Do you need a bachelor's degree for this position?"* ask *"What type of education is required for this type of position?"*

14. **Appear self-centered rather than employer-centered:** Too many job seekers still conduct one-dimensional, self-centered conversations—they want to know what the employer will do for them rather than communicate what they will do for the employer. Starting from a self-centered perspective, they ask about work loads, salaries, benefits, and vacation time. Such questions leave a poor impression on prospective employers who are interested in learning what the individual can do for them—their record and patterns of performance or examples of how they solved problems or increased productivity. They want to know why they should hire you. Effective tele-searchers keep focused on the needs of their audience and reiterate what it is they can and will do for the employer. Instead of asking *"What does this position pay?"* or *"How many hours am I expected to work each week?"*, they ask *"What do you see as my major responsibilities?"*, *"What would you like to see done that is not currently being done in this position?"*, or *"Whom would I be working with and how would they like to best work with me?"*

15. **Fail to reveal their strengths in relation to the employer's needs:** Employers have specific needs they want met through their new hirees. Candidates need to do a complete self-assessment of what they do well and enjoy doing (their strengths) and constantly communicate those strengths to employers. They can do this by constantly reiterating, through the use of strong action verbs and nouns, those actions that best represent their strengths.

16. **Call at the wrong time.** Try to avoid calling on Monday, Friday, or mid-day. These are usually the busiest times to catch most people. In many businesses, Monday mornings and Fridays are hectic. If you call between 11:30am and 2:00pm, chances are people are in meetings or out to lunch.

Good calling times tend to be between 8:00am and 10:00am and between 3:30pm and 6:00pm. The earlier and later the better. For many people, no time is a good time. You'll have to leave messages and hope it will elicit a return call.

17. **Hang up on voice mail messages.** Many people still do not know how to handle voice mail. You waste time and effort if you hang up without leaving a message. Always be prepared to leave a message designed to elicit a return call.

18. **Leave an incomplete voice mail message.** Always remember that the person using voice mail is probably a very busy person who must sort through numerous messages, prioritize them, and decide which ones deserve a return call. If you only leave your name and phone number, chances are your call will receive low priority and you many never hear from the individual. After all, who are you? You must leave enough information to motivate the individual to return your call. Also, make sure you communicate competently when leaving a message. That means using good grammar and diction and avoiding vocalized pauses and negatives. If you are nervous about leaving an impromptu message, because you may sound incompetent, hang up. Prepare a coherent and competent message and then call again and leave it on the voice mail. It is a good idea to repeat your name and phone number at the end of the message.

19. **Talk too much—or too little.** If you talk too much, your listener will probably want to avoid you in future conversations. Appearing verbally aggressive, employers will not be anxious to see you face-to-face. Indeed, talking too much is one of the deadly sins committed by many job seekers. Talking too little tends to create awkward situations and may communicate your lack of preparation or depth of knowledge. Make sure you plan your telephone conversations sufficiently so you know what you should or should not say over the telephone.

20. **Become too familial over the phone.** While you want to communicate your "likability," make sure you do not make

the mistake of becoming too friendly and personal with
telephone strangers by immediately using the person's first
name, talking like old friends, and joking a great deal. You
need to be respectful, tactful, and professional during initial
encounters. It's only after you have established a good
professional and personal relationship that you can take
familial liberties when communicating.

21. **Sound like a stereotypical salesperson who just completed
    another training session that taught them canned cold
    calling techniques.** Stereotypical cold callers tend to use the
    same old lines—*"Can I talk to the owner, or the manager,
    or the head of _____ department?" "Do you want
    to save more money?" "What would you say if I told you
    that....?"* Such canned lines tend to be immediate turn-offs
    for people who know exactly who is behind them. People
    using these canned lines tend to be pests who will waste
    your time. They deserve all the rejections they get!

22. **Give too much information and thereby eliminate
    yourself from consideration.** This is often a problem
    associated with individuals who talk too much, fail to plan
    what they should say over the telephone, and confuse their
    personal and professional lives. Do not volunteer information
    that should be reserved for a face-to-face interview or which
    might appear as a negative. Indeed, we are continuously
    surprised how many jobs seekers, especially women, volun-
    teer information that would be considered answers to illegal
    questions if asked by employers. When asked about them-
    selves, feeling a need to be up-front and honest, many
    women volunteer their age, marital status, family situation,
    spouse's occupation, daycare needs, and financial informa-
    tion—personal information that may indicate they will
    become a burden to the employer who does not have enough
    benefits to offer such a needy and potentially unstable
    employee! While such honesty may be admired by some, it
    may eliminate many people from future consideration.

23. **Fail to get through gatekeepers.** Gatekeepers come in
    several forms—operators, receptionists, secretaries, co-

workers, and voice mail. You should learn some basic communication techniques on how to get through such gatekeepers.

24. **Fail to connect your telephone call with a specific benefit for the other person.** The most effective tele-search calls are ones that connect your value to the needs of others. Always think in terms of **benefits** you have to offer others who should be motivated to listen to your message. What is it you have to offer them that would make them want to talk with you and provide you with job information, advice, and referrals? If you can't clearly answer this question, perhaps you need to rethink your telephone approach.

25. **Say honest but stupid things.** People say the darnest things when looking for a job—*"I'm looking for a job. Can you help me?"* That question will quickly create distance between you and those in your tele-search. In the job search, saying the right thing at the right time can make the difference between being accepted or rejected for a job. Be careful what you say and how you say it. You must be honest throughout your job search, but you should never volunteer negatives that might be held against you (*"I was fired from two previous jobs"* or *"I didn't like my last boss—she was a real jerk!"*). There is a difference between being honest and stupid. You need to know the difference—one is positive, the other is negative.

26. **Use awkward or silly introductions.** Many people talk like they write—unclear and lack focus. You should clearly state in your introduction who you are and why you are calling. Avoid canned sales openers which indicate you are trying to sell something. Your goals should center on gathering information, advice, and referrals or you want to influence the selection process with a follow-up call.

27. **Fail to properly close conversation with a request for action or follow-up.** Closings are just as important as openers. Most of your tele-search activities should result in some type of action or outcome. Closings should encompass

more than the obligatory "Thank you" and "good-bye."
Action closings can come in many different forms:

"May I send you a copy of my resume?"

*"If I don't hear from you by next Friday, would it be
okay if I called your office to inquire about my application?"*

*"Do you know any other people who might be able
to provide me with information on this type of position?"*

*"Where would you suggest I look for vacancies in
this area?"*

28. **Close an interview without making a follow-up telephone
call.** Most job interviews are not finished until you are
either accepted or rejected for a job. Once you complete a
job interview, be sure to follow-up with a telephone call
inquiring about the status of your candidacy. In fact, one of
the final things you should do in closing a job interview is
to ask the interviewer when the final decision will be made
and if it would be okay for you to call, if you have not
heard, within a few days after that concerning your status.
Then be sure to make this critical follow-up call. Indeed,
many job seekers report that the post-interview follow-up
call was the key to landing their job! If conducted properly,
such a call indicates your thoughtfulness and continuing
interest in the employer and the position.

29. **Project a dull or annoying telephone voice.** Your telephone voice is different from your face-to-face voice. Make
sure your telephone voice projects intelligence, energy, and
enthusiasm—key qualities employers seek in candidates and
which are communicated both over the telephone and in
face-to-face interviews. Since your first interview will
probably be conducted over the telephone as a screening
interview, it's very important that your telephone voice
communicate these key qualities.

30. **Fail to use an answering machine or enlist an answering service:** If you are a busy person who is often away from your phone, be sure you can be contacted by phone. You may want to use an answering machine or enlist a professional answering service so that you do not miss critical calls.

31. **Develop an inappropriate message for an answering machine:** If you use an answering machine, make sure you record your best professional message. No wild music, cartoon characters, or humorous lines in your message. No barking dogs, crying children, clanging dishes, or radio/TV in the background. Such background noise says more about you than the actual message you leave. And employers may not find your message as humorous as you do. Keep your message short and simple:

    "Sorry I'm unable to take your call at present. Please leave your name, number, and a message at the sound of the tone. I'll return your call as soon as possible."

    Check your messages regularly and return calls in a timely manner. Alternatively, you might consider contracting with a professional answering service to take your messages. Leaving a message with a real person is more impressive than leaving a taped message.

32. **Use the fax when a telephone call, letter, or face-to-face meeting would be more appropriate:** Faxes are a convenient communication medium for quickly transmitting written messages. Some people have become addicted to sending faxes when, instead, they should be making telephone calls or writing letters. Keep your faxes to a minimum when conducting a job search. You can best demonstrate your communication skills in letters, over the telephone, or in face-to-face meetings. Our general principle for using faxes in a job search is this: send faxes only upon request and use an informative and attractive cover sheet. Most fax requests will probably be for a copy of your resume. Include a cover letter when faxing your resume.

33. **Use the wrong kind of fax cover sheet:** Your fax cover sheet should be both attractive and informative, include your name, address, telephone and fax numbers, and the number of pages being faxed. Avoid juvenile cover sheets which may not be appreciated by your recipient. Similar to letters, your faxes should project your best professional image.

34. **Fail to follow-up fax messages with hard copy:** Always send by mail a hard copy of your faxes. Either type or handwrite in the upper left hand corner the fact that the copy was faxed on a particular date: Faxed 7/21/95. You may wish to use a yellow highlighter through the date it was faxed. This calls the reader's attention to the fact this is a hard copy of a fax. Sending this hard copy ensures that your message was received. In addition, it reminds the recipient of your earlier communication and presents it in a different, and hopefully more attractive, medium. This type of redundancy in the job search can have positive outcomes.

35. **Spend too much time looking for jobs on the information highway:** By all means use it, but don't get seduced by it! At present electronic databases and telecommunication systems are at their infancies in terms of conducting an effective job search. Like most self-proclaimed "revolutions," this one tends to be highly overstated and overrated in terms of use and effectiveness. We recommend spending no more than 15 percent of your time conducting your job search via these electronic systems. Most employers do not use them, and most systems are designed for conducting a national or international job search. Most systems are designed for recruiting technical personnel or individuals with hard-to-find skills. The use of letters, the telephone, and face-to-face meetings will probably prove to be the most useful communication mediums for your job search.

TEST YOUR TELE-SEARCH IQ

How well prepared are you for conducting an effective tele-search campaign? Let's begin testing your level of potential tele-search effectiveness by responding to the following statements:

INSTRUCTIONS: Respond to each statement by circling which number at the right best represents your situation.

SCALE: 1 = strongly agree   4 = disagree
2 = agree   5 = strongly disagree
3 = maybe, not certain

1. I enjoy using the telephone for getting
   job information, advice, and referrals.   1 2 3 4 5

2. I look forward to making ten cold calls
   a day to prospective employers.   1 2 3 4 5

3. As part of my introduction, I usually
   make a personal connection between
   myself and the person I'm calling.   1 2 3 4 5

4. I would rather call a stranger than
   write a letter to a stranger.   1 2 3 4 5

5. I'm good at meeting strangers and
   sustaining interesting conversations
   with them.   1 2 3 4 5

6. I usually plan the jist of what I will
   say over the telephone, from beginning
   to end.   1 2 3 4 5

7. I've devoted 60 percent of my job
   search time to working the telephone.   1 2 3 4 5

8. I have a clear tele-search plan for
   developing 25 new job search contacts
   each week.   1 2 3 4 5

9. I keep good records of my tele-search
   calls and follow-up accordingly.   1 2 3 4 5

10. I speak in clear sentences, use good
grammar and diction, avoid vocalized
pauses and fillers, use the active
voice, and avoid tentative, indecisive,
and negative terms.   1 2 3 4 5

11. I regularly follow-up my written
communication and interviews with
a phone call.   1 2 3 4 5

12. I'm proficient at both sending and
receiving faxes.   1 2 3 4 5

13. I usually follow-up my faxes with
hard-copy.   1 2 3 4 5

14. I conduct 95 percent of my
informational interviews over
the phone.   1 2 3 4 5

15. I know how to get past telephone
gatekeepers.   1 2 3 4 5

16. I know how to get the name of the
party I need to contact.   1 2 3 4 5

17. I know the best days of the week
and the best times of the day to
make tele-search calls.   1 2 3 4 5

18. I leave voice mail messages that
usually result in returned phone calls.   1 2 3 4 5

19. I have a clear idea of what job search
activities I need to conduct over the
telephone rather than through the mail
or in face-to-face meetings.   1 2 3 4 5

20. My telephone voice projects energy,
intelligence, and enthusiasm.   1 2 3 4 5

21. Most people enjoy talking with me
    over the phone.   1 2 3 4 5

22. I'm careful in what I say over the
    phone; I'm not one to ramble on and
    on and on.   1 2 3 4 5

23. I subscribe to one of the major tele-
    communications services (CompuServe,
    Prodigy, America Online) and regularly
    explore job opportunities on their e-mail,
    career center, or Internet options.   1 2 3 4 5

24. I can be contacted by telephone 24-
    hours a day since I use an answering
    machine, beeper, or answering service,
    or a combination of the three.   1 2 3 4 5

25. My answering machine message is
    simple and short and presents a good
    professional image.   1 2 3 4 5

You can calculate your overall tele-search effectiveness by adding the numbers you circled for a composite score. If your total is more than 75 points, you need to work on developing your tele-search skills. Your score on each item will indicate the extent to which work is needed to improve specific tele-search skills. If your score is under 50 points, you are well on your way toward tele-search effectiveness. In either case, this book should help you better develop key tele-search skills for conducting an effective job search.

3

103 DYNAMITE TELE-SEARCH TIPS AND STRATEGIES

*I*f you want to become an effective telephone communicator, you should follow several principles of effective telephone and tele-search communication. The following 103 tips and strategies help overcome the fear of using the telephone to contact strangers as well as focus on what works and what doesn't work. Taken together, they provide a complete roadmap for turning your telephone into one of your most effective job search tools.

FEARS AND PHOBIAS

If giving a speech is the number one phobia for most people, using the telephone to establish a relationship with strangers must not be far behind. Most people would rather write a letter to a stranger, or avoid them altogether, than contact them by telephone or in face-to-face situations. They fear appearing awkward, saying the wrong things, or making embarrassing mistakes.

On the other hand, some people love to meet strangers and initiate cold telephone calls. What is it they do that others don't? The remainder of this chapter, as well as the rest of this book, outlines what many of these successful telephone communicators do.

THE EFFECTIVE TELE-SEARCHER

Success

1. **The telephone is a two-edged sword.** If handled properly, the telephone can generate numerous job search rewards. Unfortunately, few job seekers are effective telephone users, especially when it comes to calling strangers who can be important to their job search. Many of these people shy away from using the telephone. They, instead, rely on sending letters and resumes through the mail. Without a well organized and focused tele-search campaign, their job search is likely to flounder, requiring twice as much time to successfully complete.

2. **Success is normally just a few more phone calls away.** Too many people never begin or prematurely quit using the telephone because of tele-search anxiety. After receiving a few rejections or encountering many gatekeepers or voice mail systems, they quit in frustration. However, such seeming impediments are all part of the tele-search game. A typical job search involves numerous rejections and incomplete starts. If you plan to be successful, you simply must continue making more phone calls and encountering more rejections and gatekeepers. Always think in probability terms: the more calls you make, the higher the probability of encountering acceptances and going beyond gatekeepers and voice mail systems. Expect a five percent accep-

tance rate—perhaps higher if you incorporate many tele-search tips outlined in this book. Many people—as many as thirty percent—will even call you back based on the messages you leave with gatekeepers and on voice mail systems!

3. **Successful telephone communicators know how they sound over the telephone because they have listened to themselves conducting telephone conversations.** People who assume they already are good telephone communicators probably haven't listened to themselves over the telephone. You might want to tape record a telephone conversation just to hear how you sound as well as communicate over the telephone. Many people who do so discover they have unusually high-pitched voices, make grammatical errors, say things that could be better phrased, or talk too fast or too slowly. Listen to yourself before you draw conclusions about your tele-search skills. Many people learn to modify their telephone skills based on such feedback.

Attitude

4. **Always maintain a positive, up-beat attitude.** Your attitude may be your most important resource in finding and keeping a job. In fact, many employers consider attitude to be more important to getting and keeping a job than technical qualifications. Employees with positive attitudes tend to work well with others, take initiative, and are willing to learn new skills. If you approach your job search with a negative attitude, chances are you will conduct a negative job search. You will communicate the wrong messages to employers who are attracted to individuals who demonstrate positive attitudes. We know developing and maintaining a positive attitude is easier said than done, especially when you encounter rejections during your job search. However, you simply must maintain a positive attitude in all of your communication encounters—in letters, over the telephone, or in face-to-face meetings.

5. **Make sure your telephone voice communicates the right attitude.** Your attitude shows when you speak. Be sure to check your telephone voice. Even though you may have a positive, up-beat attitude and your communication reflects this in letters and

in face-to-face situations, your telephone voice may not communicate such an attitude. You may need to inject more enthusiasm in your telephone conversations, improve your timing, or ask and answer questions with interesting substance. Call a friend and have him or her give you feedback on how positive you tend to communicate over the telephone. Do you sound like someone others would really enjoy talking with over the phone as well as in person?

Motivation

6. **You must remain motivated throughout your job search.** Similar to maintaining a positive attitude, keeping motivated throughout your job search can be difficult. You will experience numerous highs and lows, encounter rejections along with acceptances, and often feel less than successful in what you are doing. Job finding can be an exhausting, ego-deflating experience filled with numerous self doubts and feelings of inadequacy. But there are certain things you can do in order to keep yourself motivated and on target. Keep your self esteem high with a positive, can-do attitude. Don't take rejections personally; after all, you are involved in a probability game—you increase your chances of getting a job by increasing your job search activities. Be sure to build rewards into your job search schedule. For example, while your job search should be a seven day a week endeavor, reward yourself with a day off for every fifty tele-search activities you complete. Treat yourself to dinner at your favorite restaurant for every two job interviews you land. Developing a system of rewards tied to a schedule of projected milestones will help you both maintain a positive attitude and keep motivated throughout your job search.

7. **Your motivation shows when approaching others for job search assistance.** Too many job seekers approach others with the wrong motivations—to exploit them for information, advice, and job leads. They view networking and informational interviews as ways to persuade others to give them a job. Always remember that other people are your most precious resource when looking for employment. While most people will be happy to give you information, advice, and referrals, few want to be put

on the spot of giving you a job. Whatever you do, don't approach others for the ostensible purpose of wanting job search advice but in reality try to exploit them for a job. Your motivations will show and you will quickly become persona non grata. You must be honest and sincere in your dealings with others. Treat others as you would have them treat you. When in doubt, offer benefits to others; become employer-centered rather than self-centered in your job search approach.

Goals

8. **Set goals.** You should have a clear idea of what you want and where you are going. Without these, you will present a confusing and indecisive image to others. Clear goals help direct your job search into productive channels. Moreover, setting high goals will help make you work hard in getting what you want. Your basic tele-search goal should be the same as your job search goal—get interviews that turn into job offers.

9. **Make sure your goals are employer-centered rather than self-centered.** Goals come in many different forms. Most job seekers formulate their goals in self-centered terms—they seek to land a good job which comes with excellent salary and benefits. On the other hand, employers want your goals to relate to their needs—be productive and **add value** to their operations. When communicating with employers, make sure your goals are employer-centered—your goal is to use your skills for improving the organization's bottom line. If asked over the telephone or in an interview about your short- and long-term goals, make sure you state them in employer-centered rather than self-centered terms.

10. **Operationalize your goals into specific tele-search activities.** Setting goals is easy. But translating goals into specific day-to-day job search activities that have specific outcomes is the real challenge. If your goal is to land three job interviews next week, then you must outline a set of job search activities that should lead to that goal. At the very minimum, you will want to make at least twenty telephone calls each day in the process of gathering information, advice, and referrals. You will also want

to mail or fax at least five resumes each day. If you make fewer than 100 calls or send fewer than twenty-five resumes each week, don't expect to achieve your job search goals. You simply must translate your goals into discrete daily job search activities that contribute to the accomplishment of your goals. The failure to operationalize job search goals is one of the most important reasons for job search failure and disappointments.

Focus

11. **Keep focused on your job search goals.** A sure way to make your job search more difficult than it need be is to fail to keep focused on your goals. Indeed, many job seekers quickly get distracted with wishful thinking. Not knowing what they should focus on, they jump from one job idea or technique to another or apply for jobs unrelated to their skills and experience. In most cases this lack of focus is due to a failure to do first things first—assess interests and skills and formulate them into a clear employer-centered job objective. When you communicate with employers, make sure you stay focused on your goals. Employers want to know what it is you can do for them—your skills and abilities as they relate to their needs.

Etiquette

12. **Observe proper telephone etiquette.** Etiquette affects all phases of telephone use, from initially making a call to closing the conversation. When you make a call, start by identifying who you are and why you are calling. Be polite, considerate, and tactful. Ask intelligent questions and be a good listener. Remember, you are taking someone's time, and time is money to many busy people. Always express your gratitude for the person's time by thanking them for their assistance. If you call for information, advice, and referrals, you essentially are asking for free counseling. If you call and the person is not available, leave a message with sufficient information identifying who you are and the reason for your call. Try to find a good time to call back again and mention that you will call back at a specific time. And do call at that time. Assume busy people don't have time to return calls from strangers, especially if it is a long distance call. People

who only leave their name and telephone number often do not get their calls returned because they are suspected of being salespeople making cold calls. You must leave sufficient information to motivate strangers to call you back. Sometimes you may need to make seven telephone calls in order to get through to the person you wish to speak with. Be polite but persistent in making these repeat calls.

13. **Address strangers by their surname.** People like polite, considerate, and somewhat deferential people who observe proper social graces. When calling someone you don't know socially or professionally, address them as Mister or Miss. If you address a stranger by his or her first name, you may appear too aggressive or place yourself on an equal social plane, which may or may not be appropriate given your situation.

Personality

14. **Make your personality shine over the telephone.** You want to appear interesting and likable whether on the telephone or in face-to-face situations. Interesting and likable people have personalities that appeal to strangers. They speak with enthusiasm and intelligence. They make others want to listen to them, engage in a rewarding conversation, and meet them in person. Make sure your telephone personality exudes enthusiasm, intelligence, and energy. By all means avoid reading prepared telephone scripts!

15. **Your telephone personality should communicate a major strength sought by employers.** Employers seek individuals who demonstrate good communication skills. You must communicate well over the telephone. Verbal mistakes, from grammatical to vocalized pauses, can kill your chances of getting an interview or receiving job search assistance. Such errors stereotype you as a personality who should be avoided.

Preparation

16. **Preparation is the basis for experiencing good luck in the job search.** Successful job seekers are prepared to take advantage of

opportunities that come their way. The lucky ones tend to put themselves in many places at many times. They do this by constantly making numerous job contacts by phone, through the mail, or in face-to-face meetings.

17. **Critical telephone calls require detailed preparation.** If you know a telephone call will be important to your job search, make sure you prepare for that call. Outline exactly what points you need to cover and preferably in what sequence. Check off each item as you cover it in the conversation. Also, make notes on how you will introduce yourself as well as close the conversation. If you fail to prepare, you may forget to cover important points. Such lost opportunities are unfortunate since you may not have a chance to talk to the person again. And you don't want to call back and mention you forgot to ask a few questions—that would make you appear disorganized and unprepared.

18. **Don't prepare by memorizing or reading your message.** Similar to giving a speech, your conversation should be based on preparation which includes points you need to cover. Cover your points in an impromptu manner. Preparation should never include memorizing or reading what you want to say. Anything memorized or read is likely to sound canned and insincere—real "killers" in a job search.

Organization

19. **Organize your job search and initiate your telephone activities around an interrelated seven-step process.** When using the telephone, keep in mind exactly where you are in the job search process. The job search follows a well-defined seven-step sequential process involving these steps:

    1. Assessing interests and skills
    2. Setting an objective
    3. Researching jobs and employers
    4. Writing resumes and letters
    5. Networking
    6. Interviewing
    7. Negotiating salary and terms of employment

While the telephone gets used most frequently during the networking phase, it also is used during the other phases. You especially will want to use it for conducting research and following-up your resume, letter writing, and interviewing activities.

20. **Within each job search step, organize your activities over a specific yet realistic time frame.**

Most job seekers have unrealistic expectations about how long it will take to find a job. Successful job seekers expect to spend three to six months before connecting with a suitable job. You are well advised to spend two weeks putting together a powerful resume and another two weeks researching jobs, employers, and companies. You should constantly make phone calls throughout your job search—from day one to the very last day.

21. **Don't organize too much.** Too much organization can kill serendipity—chance occurrences that often turn into new opportunities. Organize yourself, but keep your eye open for unexpected opportunities. Reorganize when necessary in order to take advantage of those opportunities. Your organization should be flexible enough to permit new and unexpected opportunities to arise throughout your job search.

Target Audience

22. **Always direct your calls to a specific person rather than to a position or a process.** The more you can personalize your communication, the higher the probability you will get what you want. Try to get the name of the person you need to speak to before you contact them directly. If you make a cold call to speak with the person by first asking *"Who makes the hiring decisions in Personnel,"* you are likely to be screened out as a "cold caller." Try calling first to get the name of the right person you need to speak to and then make another call in which you ask for that person by name. Saying

"Hi, this is Jane Bellington calling for John Tate in Personnel."

is much more effective than saying

> *"Can you connect me with the person who makes the hiring decisions in Personnel?"*

The first approach is likely to get you through to the person. The second approach is likely to get you screened out by a gatekeeper who recognizes canned lines used by cold callers.

23. **Indicate your intelligence and initiative with prior knowledge of the individual and/or the organization**. Do your research **before** you make a telephone call. Connect yourself to the individual and/or organization by indicating that you are familiar with their position or operations. Avoid asking basic questions that indicate you haven't done your research, such as *"What do you do? What kind of products does this company produce? How many people do you employ?"* You need to communicate your intelligence and initiative rather than waste potential employers' time with questions that indicate your ignorance and lack of prior research and initiative.

Voice Mail

24. **Expect to encounter voice mail with at least fifty percent of your calls.** More and more people in all types and sizes of organizations use voice mail to collect, screen, and retrieve their messages. When you make a phone call, expect to leave a message on voice mail rather than communicate directly with the individual you are calling. Many voice mail systems put you directly through to the individual's mail box whereas other systems may first route you through an operator or give you an operator option. If you have an operator option, ask the operator when you might best be able to contact the individual directly. He or she may be able to suggest a good time to call back. At the same time, leave a message in the individual's mail box.

25. **Be sure to leave an informative message that is likely to result in a return call.** People who use voice mail tend to be busy people who must screen which calls they will return. At least thirty percent of voice mail messages can be disregarded with

little or no consequences. Many of these messages are cold calls
intended to solicit business and acquire information. Make sure
your message does not get screened into that thirty percent! Your
message should state the following: (1) purpose of your call, (2)
the best time to contact you, and (3) your phone number. If you
fail to clearly state your purpose, you may be screened out as a
potential nuisance call. In your statement of purpose, try to
connect yourself to the individual's interests. For example,

Referral Connection

"Jim Carlson suggested I call you about your work at ..."

Cold Call

*"This is Janice Wilson at 717-234-1100. I'm calling in
reference to your work in computer sales."*

Expand your statement to include a complete message. A cold
call message might include the following:

*"Hi, this is Emily Zeiber. I'm calling about your innova-
tive work in graphic design. It's now 1:45pm. I'll be in
until 6:00pm today and all day tomorrow. My number is
221-4941. I look forward to speaking with you soon."*

26. **Use your own voice mail, an answering machine, an answering service, a beeper, or e-mail if you are difficult to contact
by phone.** Looking for a job requires constant communication
within an ever expanding network. Since you will be making
numerous phone calls in developing your job search network,
make sure you can be easily contacted. If someone returns your
call and gets no answer or no opportunity to leave a message,
don't expect that person to call you back again. Returning a call
once is sufficient for most people who know little or nothing
about you and the purpose of your call. At the very minimum
you should use an answering machine or some form of voice
mail. If you use the Internet or one of the commercial electronic
communication systems, you may want to use your e-mail
address in your job search.

Leaving Messages

27. **Your message should motivate the receiver to return your call immediately.** Most individuals prioritize which messages they will return. Your message should sufficiently grab the attention of the receiver to call you back immediately.

28. **Your message should clearly state who you are and the nature of your call.** Be clear and purposeful when leaving messages. Nothing is more irritating than to listen to a message that only includes a name and phone number. If the person does not know who you are or why they should call you back, chances are they will screen out your call. They may assume you are trying to make a cold call to sell them something—calls they wish to avoid!

29. **Your message should ask the receiver to take action—return your call as soon as possible.** Again, leaving only a name and telephone number is an incomplete message. Since you want action, your message must call for action. You have two choices here. First, leave a message in which you ask the individual to call you back at such-and-such a time. Second, leave a message in which you indicate you plan to call back at such-and-such a time.

Repeating Calls

30. **Don't give up if you can't get through to the person or your phone messages are not immediately returned.** There are many reasons why individuals do not return their calls. One of the major reasons relates to the quality of the message left for them—it's incomplete or fails to motivate the person to take action. Other reasons might be the person is out of town, ill, or preoccupied with important business. They have immediate priorities that need to be taken care of before returning their phone calls. Don't assume someone is not returning your call because they don't want to talk with you. More likely they have other reasons for not calling you.

31. **Persistence eventually pays off.** Too many people give up prematurely after experiencing a few rejections. Don't let this

happen to you. If after making seven calls and you still can't get through to the person or your messages to return your call are disregarded, ask a third party to intervene on your behalf (*"Could you give her a call for me please?"*) or write a letter in which you indicate you have been unsuccessful in getting through to the person but still *"wish to talk to her concerning...."* In ninety percent of the cases such persistence results in getting through to the person. However, too many people give up after making only two or three calls. Six unreturned calls and messages will usually make the individual feel guilty for not returning your calls. Such guilt often translates into a return call along with an apology for not returning your call sooner. However, be careful about conducting an "in your face" tele-search campaign by constantly pestering a person. Know when it's time to ease up and move on to more productive contacts.

Handling Gatekeepers

32. **You will encounter many gatekeepers in your tele-search campaign.** Recognize this as a fact of job search life and deal with it as an important tele-search challenge. Remember, gatekeepers have an important job to perform—screen people in and out of further communication with their bosses or colleagues. While they deserve professional respect, they should not be viewed as insurmountable obstacles. You need to develop an effective strategy for handling these gatekeepers.

33. **Treat gatekeepers with respect and professionalism**. They often serve as the eyes and ears of those who make hiring decisions. In many cases you may actually establish a friendly relationship with the gatekeeper who will promote you to their boss. This frequently happens after leaving several messages with the gatekeeper to have his or her boss return your call. After your sixth call the gatekeeper may personally intervene on your behalf—but only if you have treated this person with respect, professionalism, and hopefully a good sense of humor. Whatever you do, don't alienate a gatekeeper by treating them as an inferior. After all, they are one of your most important windows to opportunity.

Answering Machines

34. You must make yourself available during regular business hours. The easiest and most cost effective method for making yourself available is to attach an answering machine or voice mail program to your telephone line. Your message should be simple and to the point—that you are not available at present but you will return the call as soon as possible. If you plan to be out of town for a few days, change your message to indicate that you will be gone until such and such a time. If you travel a lot, you should invest in an answering machine that allows you to retrieve your messages from different locations. Not being available at critical times is a sure way to kill your job search.

35. Use a good quality answering machine or voice mail program for recording and retrieving messages. Good quality answering machines are relatively inexpensive as are many computerized voice mail systems. At a very minimum, your machine or program should record the date and time of each message received, enable callers to leave a message up to two or three minutes, and let you retrieve messages by remote from other locations.

36. Your answering machine message should be short, informative, and professional. Avoid long and irritating messages. Don't waste more than ten seconds of a listener's time with your message. Keep it short, succinct, and cheery:

> *"Sorry I missed your call. Please leave your name, telephone number, and a message at the sound of the tone. I'll return your call as soon as possible. Thanks for calling."*

Longer messages can be irritating to a caller who is anxious to immediately get to the beep in order to leave a name and phone number. Do not use humorous prerecorded messages which may question both your intelligence and professionalism. They probably will not be interpreted in a positive manner by the caller who is making a serious call. Be sure to inject personality and enthusiasm into your message. After all, this may be your first voice encounter with a potential employer!

Returning Calls

37. **Return your calls as soon as possible**. Don't delay in returning phone messages. The sooner you get back to the caller, the sooner you will make a positive impression as someone who returns his calls immediately. And telephone impressions and etiquette do count in the job search. How you handle yourself in using the telephone gives others clues about your competence and likability.

38. **Immediately identify yourself when you return a call.** Assuming you are likely to encounter a gatekeeper when making a return call, your returned call should be received by a gatekeeper as one which should be immediately recognized. When you return a call, immediately state why you are calling. For example:

    "Hi, this is Jane Bellington returning John Tate's call."

    Such a statement immediately identifies you as someone who has priority is speaking directly with the gatekeeper's boss.

Answering Calls

39. **Answer your phone by immediately identifying yourself.** Avoid answering a call by just saying *"Hello."* Such a greeting forces the caller to ask a question—*"I'm calling for Jim Wells. Is he in?"* or *"Is Jim Wells available?"* Immediately identify yourself by saying, *"Jim Wells speaking."* The caller can then state his or her business—*"This is Mary Case returning your call."*

40. **Be prepared to handle a variety of important job search calls.** While you may be prepared to leave good messages for people who are unavailable when you call, you should be equally prepared to answer the phone when the person returns your call. Since you may be calling dozens of people, you may have difficulty remembering whom you called and left a message for. Keep your telephone records near the phone so you can quickly refer to your notes when people return their call. Immediately

write down their name and turn to your records so you can jog your memory about the nature of the call. Indeed, it's embarrassing to answer the phone and forget who the person is and why you called them. Keep a list of questions you want to ask with your telephone records. Above all, you want to sound well organized and purposeful in your telephone conversation.

41. **Don't try to conduct a job interview over the phone.** Job interviews are best conducted in face-to-face settings. The purpose of a phone call should be to get information you can use for your job search. If your telephone conversation turns into a telephone interview, you may be ill prepared to deal with many questions that are best handled in a face-to-face meeting.

Using Humor

42. **Lighten up!** While the job search is serious business for both you and potential employers, it should not be dreadfully serious nor become a heavy burden for others. Since likability is one of the most important characteristics sought by employers, you can express your likability by injecting a sense of humor and personality in your dealings with others. Employers appreciate a sense of humor in employees. If you don't do it at present, learn to occasionally smile and laugh. But don't overdue it by trying to be overly funny or tell inappropriate jokes. Your sense of humor should express your personality, intelligence, and competence. Above all, it tells others that you are someone they will like working with.

Fielding Objections

43. **Expect to encounter objections to your qualifications.** Since you are a stranger to the many people you encounter in your job search, expect these people to be suspicious of you, your qualifications, and your motivations. Whether or not they directly verbalize their suspicions, many of these people will raise objections to you as a potential employee. They suspect you have weaknesses which should disqualify you from employment with them and their organizations.

44. Be prepared to handle objections. Objections can come in many forms. Some people may be unwilling to give you information and referrals. Others may object to you as a candidate for a job. Be prepared to turn such objections into positives or new opportunities. List five or ten weaknesses others are likely to have regarding your candidacy—lacks lengthy experience or training, changed jobs frequently, fired from a previous position, dropped out of college, marital status or family situation, previous salary. Know that these may be potential weaknesses and objections to your candidacy and develop some terrific responses that are positive for your candidacy. Some of these weaknesses may be raised during a telephone screening interview.

45. Turn potential weaknesses into strengths by either neutralizing an objection or turning it into a positive. You can do this by responding to an objection in four different ways. If, for example, a potential employer asks you *"What are some of your weaknesses?"*, you can respond to this question four different ways:

   A. **Discuss a negative which is not related to the job being considered:** *"I don't enjoy accounting. I know it's important, but I find it boring. Even at home my wife takes care of our books. Marketing is what I like to do. Other people are much better at bookkeeping than I am."*

   B. **Discuss a negative the person already knows:** *"I spent a great deal of time working on advanced degrees and thus I lack extensive work experience. However, I believe my education has prepared me well for this job. My leadership experience in college taught me how to work with people, organize, and solve problems. I write well and quickly. My research experience helped me analyze, synthesize, and develop strategies."*

   C. **Discuss a negative which you managed to improve upon:** *"I used to get over-committed and miss important deadlines. But then I read a book on time management and learned what I was doing wrong. Within three weeks*

I reorganized my use of time and found I could meet my deadlines with little difficulty. The quality of my work also improved. Now I have time to work out each day. I'm doing more and feeling better at the same time."

D. **Discuss a negative that can also be a positive:** *"I'm somewhat of a workaholic. I love my work, but I sometimes neglect my family because of it. I've been going into the office seven days a week, and I often put in 12 hour days. I'm now learning to better manage my time."*

Cold Calling

46. **If you want to rapidly expand your job search network, you must make many cold calls.** Whether you like it or not, you must make cold calls in order to expand your job search network. If you don't, your job search network will probably remain small. Cold calling techniques enable you to dramatically increase the number of contacts to expand your network for acquiring job information, advice, and referrals.

47. **Most people dislike making cold calls because they don't know how to best initiate such calls.** It's no secret that most people would rather initiate conversations with people they know or with whom they have a personal referral than to strangers. Indeed, most people feel uncomfortable approaching strangers. And they feel especially uncomfortable asking strangers via the telephone for personal advice or assistance. However, we all approach strangers from time to time. We ask for directions, seek information, or engage in small talk with strangers we meet in lines or at parties. Indeed, many people are excellent "networkers" because they know how to approach strangers in business and social settings and engage in purposeful small talk. Most such encounters take place in face-to-face settings and are relatively spontaneous and rewarding. But what happens when we are advised to make cold telephone calls? The same people who are comfortable meeting strangers in face-to-face settings avoid making cold calls. What they most lack is a good set of cold calling techniques that enable them to approach strangers over the telephone as easily as they approach strangers in face-to-face

settings. If you feel uncomfortable initiating small talk with strangers in face-to-face settings, refer to Anne Baber and Lynne Waymon's *Great Connections: Small Talk and Networking for Businesspeople* (Impact) and Susanne RoAne's *How to Work a Room* (Warner) for useful networking tips. Numerous books dealing with sales techniques outline telephone cold calling and prospecting techniques such as Stephan Schiffman's *Cold Calling Techniques That Really Work* (Adams Media) and Joan Guiducci's *Power Calling: A Fresh Approach to Cold Calls and Prospecting* (Tonino).

48. **Cold calling techniques work well for most job seekers.** The proof is in the outcomes. Job seekers who incorporate cold calling techniques into their job search are able to significantly enlarge the scope of their job search. Their cold calls result in an expanded network of individuals who provide information, advice, and referrals for locating quality jobs.

49. **Develop cold calling techniques that best fit your personality style.** The stereotypical, aggressive cold caller may not be a good model for you given your particular personality style. If you are relatively shy and generally avoid initiating contacts with strangers, you'll need to develop a cold calling approach that is most appropriate for your personality style.

50. **Practice cold calling scripts for opening and closing your cold calls.** Successful cold callers develop scripts for introducing themselves, motivating the listener to continue the conversation, and closing the call with a request for information, advice, and/or referrals. For example, if you are calling someone for information on job opportunities, you might introduce yourself as follows:

> *"Hi, this is John Adams calling. We've not met, but I've heard many good things about your work at Mercy Hospital. I'm in the process of gathering information on hospitals in the Detroit area and thought you would be the perfect person to contact about your interests. Do you have a few minutes? I won't keep you long...."*

"Hi, this is John Adams calling. Are you the Janice Mays who has been doing the wonderful work at Parkside West? I read the article in yesterday's Post about your project. What a terrific job you've done in revitalizing the neighborhood. I'm calling because I'm interested in learning more about...."

"Hi, this is John Adams calling. Are you currently hiring for any warehouse positions? Do you anticipate any vacancies in the near future? Are you accepting applications at present?"

We cannot stress too much, however, that you should practice the jist of the message you wish to communicate. Do not try to memorize exact words.

Telephone Screening Interviews

51. **Many job search calls automatically turn into telephone screening interviews.** Even though you may only be calling for information, advice, or referrals, chances are the person at the other end of the telephone is evaluating you as a potential candidate; their evaluation screens you in many different ways—from volunteering information to inviting you to an interview. The degree to which they volunteer information and advice will depend on their evaluation of your personality and competence. If you are too aggressive and pushy, they may close the door on you immediately by being courteous but uncooperative. If they instantly like you, they may volunteer a great deal of useful information, advice, and referrals. Employers screen in a different manner but the principle of "liking you" remains the same. Most employers will conduct a telephone screening interview before inviting you to a formal job interview.

52. **Be prepared to conduct a telephone screening interview at any time.** An employer may call you at any time—you may be in the shower, eating breakfast, or in the middle of an important meeting. Just assume you may get such calls at odd times. One of the best ways to prepare is to keep a list of questions handy that you need to ask during a screening interview. Remember,

while the employer may be screening you over the telephone, you should be screening the employer at the same time. After all, you don't want to waste your time going to a job interview with an employer who does not meet your expectations. Now is the time to ask some key employer screening questions. You should have at least five questions prepared for this interview. Keep your answers and questions focused on your objective: you're looking for a position related to your interests and skills. Avoid any questions concerning salary and benefits. These questions are best handled at the very end of a job interview—after you have had a chance to establish your value in relation to the position.

53. **Send a thank you letter after completing a telephone screening interview.** You want to be remembered by many people you encounter during your job search. And thoughtful individuals are **remembered** by employers because they write thank you letters.

Referral Calls

54. **Referral calls should be your most effective tele-search activity.** The purpose of a referral call is to get more information and referrals to advance your job search. These calls are the easiest to make since you will have the name and phone number of someone who knows someone you know. In many cases, someone will recommend that you call a relative, friend, or professional associate who will be willing to assist you. Such a contact gives you easy access to this referral. In contrast to a cold call, your contact name in a referral call gives you instant credibility. In most cases the referral will be happy to talk with you since he or she is discharging a family, friendship, or professional obligation. Expect the referral to give you frank and honest advice and, hopefully, excellent additional referrals that result in more job leads and possible interviews.

55. **Use a standard opener when making a referral call.** The best opener is to introduce yourself as an acquaintance of the referral. Immediately establish your relationship to the referral by mentioning the fact that this person was recommended to you by the mutual acquaintance. Use some form of this basic opener:

"Hi, this is Bill Watson. Maryann Stephens recommended that I call you. She said you would be a good person to talk to about . . . . "

You might follow your opener with a request for the individual's time.

"Would this be a good time to . . . ?"

"Would you have a few minutes to . . . ?"

56. **Referral calls can have several outcomes.** At the very minimum your referral call should result in more job search information and referrals. Remember, your purpose is to continue expanding your job search network. You are literally adding more eyes, ears, and advisers to your network. In some cases a referral may have little or no outcome. However, most referral calls should result in some useful information and advice. For example, the referral may give you a job lead to XYZ company, inform you of salary ranges for XYZ positions, or tell you to contact a friend who can give you more information and advice. In some cases, the referral may indicate a willingness to meet with you. He or she may even have an impending job opening for which you may qualify.

57. **Referral calls should result in more referrals.** At the very minimum, you want your referral call to result in more referrals. If nothing else results from your conversation, at least close it with some form of this standard referral line:

"Thank you very much for your time. I've learned a lot in just a few minutes talking with you. Maryann was right when she said you would be most helpful. I have one final request. Would you know two or three other individuals who might be willing to share information about jobs in the advertising field? I feel I really need to learn more about this field from people like you."

Such a closing will usually result in two or three referrals with whom you can repeat similar openings and closings.

58. **Send a nice thank you note to your referrals.** Remember, while your immediate purpose is to get useful information, advice, and referrals, you also want to be **remembered** in the coming weeks and months. One of the best ways to get remembered is to send a thank you letter in which you reiterate your appreciation for the individual's time and useful information, advice, and/or referrals. Not only is this a thoughtful thing to do, it also is the wise thing to do. This same individual may later learn about an impending job opening for which you may qualify. Your call followed up by a thank you letter may establish you as both a thoughtful and potentially qualified individual person who might be appropriate for such a position. Don't be surprised to discover this referral recommends you for the position, either by calling you directly and recommending that you contact someone about the position (a job search referral) or recommending you to the employer who, in turn, calls you directly and screens you over the telephone for a job.

Likability

59. **Tele-search activities should first and foremost establish your likability.** While employers seek competent individuals who are qualified to perform particular jobs, they also seek individuals they like. After all, they have to live with employees many hours a day. They desire smooth interpersonal relations with their employees. All else being equal, your degree of likability will probably determine how well you do in your job search.

60. **Whether you know it or not, you're being screened over the telephone for your likability.** Employers can easily screen you for job performance competency by giving you a test, checking your references and previous job performance, or interpreting your resume and application. But it's more difficult to determine your likability—your ability to get along well with the employer and co-workers. Employers must make subjective judgments based upon their telephone and face-to-face encounters with you. In fact, telephone and face-to-face interviews tend to screen more for personality and likability than for job performance competency. Will you be a team player? Do you have a friendly and cooperative personality? Do people enjoy working with you each

day? Your likability will be constantly assessed throughout your job search. Since your initial contact with referrals and employers may be by telephone, your likability will be assessed by how well you open and close the conversation, the sound of your voice, the use of humor, and your follow-up activities (Did you send a thank you letter?). How well you handle yourself over the telephone says a great deal about how well others will like you.

61. **You can make yourself more likable over the telephone by observing some basic principles of telephone etiquette.** Many people communicate awkwardly over the telephone. They use clumsy introductions and closings, fail to sustain coherent thoughts, speak so softly that hardly can be heard, or try to be funny. If they use an answering machine, they often leave an inappropriate message. Basic telephone etiquette is similar to writing a letter. At the very beginning, clearly state who you are and why you are calling. Keep the conversation focused around your goals. Use a thoughtful close. Recognize you are being screened, put your best foot forward in what you say and how you say it.

Timing

62. **The best times for making cold calls are either early morning or late afternoon on Tuesday, Wednesday, or Thursday.** Busy people tend to be disproportionately busy on Monday and Friday and throughout the day. They tend to be in meetings or with appointments between 9:00am and 12:00 noon and between 1:30pm and 4:00pm. Good times to call are between 8:00am and 9:00am and after 4:00pm. The 5:00pm to 6:00pm period may be good; many busy people stay in their offices an extra hour at the end of the day. Some come to their offices an hour earlier than their staff.

63. **Referral calls can be made at any time.** If you making a referral call to a busy person, try calling at the same times recommended for making cold calls. However, since you have a referral, you can call at any time. If the person is not available, leave a message in which you mention the person who made the referral. Chances are your call will be returned.

64. Expect to receive job-related calls at any time. Your networking and application activities will eventually turn into job interviews and offers. Be prepared to speak with prospective employers by telephone at any time. Once you initiate networking activities, employment contacts, or applications, you may receive a call from a prospective employer. Such a call is usually a screening interview—you will be asked several questions to determine whether or not to invite you to a formal job interview or a series of interviews. Keep a list of your job search contacts as well as questions you wish to ask near your phone at all times. You may not have a second chance to make a good telephone impression on employers!

65. Follow-up referrals immediately. If someone is good enough to give you a job referral, make sure you immediately follow up such a referral, preferably within 24 hours. After all, your contact may call the referral and mention to them that you will be calling shortly based on their recommendation. When you introduce yourself to the referral, you might mention that you just spoke with the contact about them. For example,

> *"Hi, this is Bill Watson. I just spoke with Maryann Stephens and she recommended that I call you about my interests in...."*

66. Always send thank you letters within 24 hours. Anyone giving you job information and referrals deserves a nice thank you letter. Someone screening you for an interview also should receive such a letter. Whatever the case, make sure you send the thank you letter within 24 hours. The sooner the individual receives such a thoughtful letter, the greater its impact. You want to be immediately remembered, especially if you've just completed a screening interview. The timeliness of your letter can make the difference between being selected or rejected for a job interview. It's especially important if you feel your telephone conversation did not go as well as you would have liked.

67. Fax requests should be responded to immediately. If someone asks you to fax them a copy of your resume or a sample of your writing, be sure to do so immediately. The longer you wait, the more likely you will be forgotten or your slow response will be interpreted in a negative manner. Quick responders make very positive impressions.

Approach

68. Select a telephone approach that best represents your unique personality and style. While it is easy to follow telephone scripts and play a role, it's important to express your unique personality and style over the phone. Telephone listeners recognize canned lines and well rehearsed or memorized scripts. You must be spontaneous is both answering and asking questions.

69. You must have an approach for both developing and following-up your contacts. Learning how to approach people and initiate conversations with strangers or referrals is only one side of the tele-search equations. Make sure you have just as good an approach for following-up your telephone conversation, from sending thank up letters to making another call.

Assertiveness

70. Don't confuse assertiveness with aggressiveness. Aggressive individuals tend to be obnoxious in the job search. Assertive individuals tend to be focused and persistent in achieving their goals. They don't give up after encountering rejections. Know the difference as you approach your job search assertively.

Voice

71. Listen to your telephone voice. When was the last time you listened to your telephone voice? You may discover your telephone voice sounds much different from your regular voice. For example, some people tend to have high pitched voices which are irritating to listeners. Have someone tape record and critique your telephone voice. Then listen to it together. Do you sound professional and interesting—someone others would like to meet in person? Do you project well over the phone? Do you need to slow down or speed up your pace? Should you raise or lower your voice? Do you sound nervous or at ease? You may discover you can greatly improve the quality of your telephone voice through some very simple voice techniques.

Grammar

72. **Grammatical mistakes can kill your candidacy.** One sign of a professional is good grammar. Listen to how your ask and answer questions. Is your grammar impeccable? Do you speak in complete sentences, user proper nouns and verbs, and speak in the active voice?

Vocalized Pauses

73. **Avoid using vocalized pauses.** Many people have the bad habit of using vocalized pauses, such as *"ah"* and *"uhm"*. Occasional vocalized pauses are okay, but if you use them excessively, your listener will become distracted from your message. Worst of all, you will sound annoying. Make a conscious effort to speak in complete sentences and punctuate with brief silent pauses rather than with annoying vocalized pauses.

Ambiguous and Negative Language

74. **Avoid using ambiguous and negative language.** You want to project a positive, energetic, and upbeat image of yourself to others. However, many people tend to use ambiguous and somewhat negative terms. If, for example, you use *"pretty good"*, *"fairly well"*, or *"maybe"*, you may sound very indecisive. While it's okay to admit that you *"don't know"* something, excessive use of ambiguous and negative language will tend to create negative impressions.

75. **Don't confess your weaknesses by using negative language.** When you talk about your interests and previous experience, avoid using negative language. For example, rather than say

   "I really didn't like college and so I dropped out during my junior year."

put this experience in more positive language:

"I completed two years of college before joining ABC Advertising Agency."

Practice using positive language when talking about interests, experience, and goals. You want to be positive, energetic, and upbeat in what you say to others. Employers like such people.

Diction

76. **Poor diction can be as deadly as poor grammar.** How well do you pronounce words? Do you sometimes mispronounce or shorten words? Which of the following do you say?

Incorrect	Correct
goin	*going*
gonna	*going to*
Adlanta	*Atlanta*
din't	*didn't*
idear	*idea*
yea	*yes*

Even many so-called educated people have sloppy or lazy speech habits. Unfortunately, except for close family members, most people are reluctant to correct others' diction errors. Instead, they may conclude you are uneducated and thus lack the ability to advance professionally. They may overlook you for a job or career advancement because of poor diction. Again, listen carefully how you pronounce words. These are habits you can easily break by being conscious of them. If you have some very bad habits, you might want to contact a voice and diction specialist who can help you improve your speech. You may discover your speech is hindering your career advancement.

Time and Talk

77. **Spend at least 60 percent of your job search time using the telephone.** The telephone is one of your most effective job search tools. It enables you to quickly develop job search

contacts, enlarge your network, conduct informational interviews, and follow-up activities. We recommend spending at least 50 percent of your time using the telephone to make cold and referral calls as well as conduct informational interviews and follow-ups. The most effective job seekers spend more than 80 percent of their job search time on the telephone.

78. **Expect to spend no more than five minutes conducting a cold call conversation.** Many people, especially busy people, are reluctant to talk with strangers. Once you've made contact, try to keep the conversation to three to five minutes. Indeed, as part of your approach to a stranger, mention that you'll only take a few minutes. If the person is willing to talk longer (not too busy at the moment), continue on. Close this short conversation with a request to talk with the person again:

> *"I really appreciate having a chance to talk with you. I know you're probably very busy. Would it be okay to call you again if I have any further questions? Is there a particularly good time to call you?"*

Now that you have established a relationship, this request will help keep the door open to future contact.

79. **Referral calls can take any length of time, depending on the nature of the conversation and the person you are talking with.** Most referrals feel an obligation to speak with you because of your contact. They normally will spend more time with you and be more helpful than your cold call contacts. If the person appears busy, be considerate and try to reschedule the call for another time:

> *"Is this a good time to talk or would another time be better?"*

Some referrals may spend ten, twenty, thirty, or more minutes on the phone with you or schedule a time to meet.

80. **Learn to know when to end a call.** Too many job seekers talk too much to the point of turning off their contacts. Indeed, one

of the deadly job interview sins is "talking too much." Before making a call, determine how long you plan to keep the person on the phone. Five to ten minutes should be sufficient. After ten minutes your call may become a burden for your contact. Time yourself and make an effort to bring the conversation to a close within that five to ten minute period. If you feel you need more time, it may be best to call back later.

Openers

81. **Use different openers for different types of calls.** Openers for tele-search calls should follow the same principles as openers for job search letters: grab the attention of your audience and identify who you are and what you want. Cold calls should begin by establishing common ground between the caller and listener— what is it they share? A common interest in a particular job field or position? Referral calls begin with common ground—both individuals share a common contact, someone who referred the caller to the listener. You will need to open each type of call with a different introduction.

82. **Your openers should express your unique personality and style.** Use openers that make you appealing to the listener, preferably one that strokes the ego and connects you with the listener. Ego strokes must be honest and not overdone. If you are making a cold call, try something like this:

> *"Are you the Mary Wilson who wrote that wonderful article on day care centers that appeared in last week's Post? I really admire the work you're doing at First Care. My name is Alicia Christian. Would you have a few minutes? I'm really interested in day care in Boston and thought you would be the best person to talk to."*

If you are using a referral, try establishing common ground in this manner:

> *"Hi, this is Matt Douglas. I just got off the phone with Jay Wilson. He strongly recommended that I call you. He said you are doing some wonderful, innovative work in multime-*

dia production that's related to my own work. Would you have a few moments to talk or is there a better time I could call back?"

83. **Avoid canned or cutesy openers.** Cold calling openers can be deadly if they are canned or cutesy. How would you respond to a job seeker who used these on you:

   "Are you looking for someone who can double your sales in six months?"

   "Would you like to make more money?"

   "Can I speak to the owner of the business?"

   These are standard cold calling sales pitches we hear every day. They immediately turn us off as mindless canned calling lines. Our first reaction is to hang up without uttering a word. These openers are sure signs the callers will waste our time trying to sell us a product we neither need nor want.

Small Talk

84. **Be prepared to engage in small talk, but keep it to a minimum.** Small talk plays a key role in developing relationships with strangers and in expanding interpersonal relationships. Develop a list of five small talk topics you feel comfortable talking about. These topics will help you break the ice in cold calls and sustain conversations that occasionally go silent. If you need practice in developing small talk approaches, we recommend reviewing Anne Baber and Lynne Waymon's *Great Connections: Small Talk and Networking for Businesspeople* (Impact).

Initiative

85. **Good job search outcomes come to those who take initiative.** Few people are fortunate enough to be in demand amongst employers—employers seek them out rather than them seeking

out employers. Eighty percent of getting a job will depend on your initiative—whom you contact, the number of cold calls you make, how often you contact prospects, your presentation skills, and your follow-up activities. The remaining twenty percent depends on luck and timing. If you want to experience the very best luck, you must take initiative in making numerous telephone calls throughout your job search. Unfortunately, most people take very little initiative. They respond to a few classified ads with resumes and cover letters and spend a lot of time worrying about their future. The lack of initiative is probably the single most important factor for job search failure.

86. **Only you can take the necessary initiative for developing your tele-search network.** While many people will give you advice and referrals, don't expect them to find you a job. You must take the initiative to follow-up on the advice and initiate telephone calls with the referrals. The best way to do this is to pick up the telephone and dial the number. Remember, you may be initiating a conversation that can have important positive consequences for your future. This may well be your $1 million call—it might result in that much in income over the next ten years!

Tactfulness

87. **You must be tactful in how you handle yourself and others over the telephone.** Let's face it. You're looking for a job. Best of all, you're looking for a job in all the right places by frequently using the telephone throughout your job search. However, be careful in how you handle yourself with contacts and employers. While you are looking for a job, do not put others on the spot by asking them for a job when making cold and referral calls. No one wants to be responsible for your employment fate! The tactful approach is to ask people for information, advice, and referrals. The only time you should directly ask for a job is when you conduct a telemarketing campaign to uncover job leads. Such a campaign is very simple in structure (see pages 115-116). You open your telephone call with some version of these two lines:

"Do you have any vacancies at present? Are you accepting applications at present?"

If you are the subject of a telephone screening interview, avoid talking about these subjects: your weaknesses, salary and benefits. The tactful approach to a telephone screening interview is to focus on the employer's goals and try to turn the telephone interview into a face-to-face interview.

Honesty

88. Be honest but don't be stupid. Honesty is always the best policy when looking for a job but it should not become a liability. Many people confuse honesty with being open, frank, and emotional and confessing negatives. As a result, they often say the dumbest things that disqualify them from further consideration. If, for example, an employer asks you why you left your last job, you can be honest without being stupid. For example, the following statement may be a very honest way of portraying your reason for leaving your last job:

> *"I really didn't like my boss. He was a real jerk who sexually harassed me. I finally went to my lawyer and we decided to sue the company. In the end, we settled out of court. I really hated that place and decided not to go back."*

But this is also a very stupid way to present your honesty. You can still be honest but tactful in how you portray your situation:

> *"While I learned a great deal and acquired excellent experience at XYX company, I advanced as far as I could in the organization. I'm looking for an opportunity with a larger firm that will allow me to fully use my training and experience in multimedia production. That's why I'm interested in your company."*

The point here is that there are many ways to verbalize honesty. You do neither yourself nor a prospective employer any good by confessing all the sordid details. In fact, you may do yourself much harm by being excessively honest.

Questions

89. **Be prepared to answer several questions that are likely to be asked over the telephone by prospective employers.** Employers who screen you over the telephone usually ask several types of questions to determine whether or not to invite you to a face-to-face interview or series of interviews. These include the following:

   - Education and training
   - Experience and qualifications
   - Interests and goals
   - Availability and commitment

   Many of the questions will focus on the content of your resume and the requirements of the position and the needs of the company. For an overview of the types of questions you are likely to encounter in an interview, see our *Interview for Success* and *Dynamite Answers to Interview Questions* (Impact).

90. **Try to tactfully avoid addressing certain questions over the phone.** In many telephone screening interviews, the interviewer will ask potentially disqualifying questions. After all, their job is to both screen in and screen out several candidates. Typical screening questions deal with your

   - Salary history, expectations, or requirements
   - Weaknesses
   - Experience
   - Willingness to travel, relocate, work overtime

   Be especially careful in how you address the salary question. Ideally you want to keep this question to the very last—at the end of your face-to-face interviews when it's time to add everything up and talk about assigning value to both you and position. If you are forced to state a salary figure, do so as a salary range and only after you turn the question around:

   "What does your company pay for someone with my experience and qualifications?"

If the interviewer is unfamiliar with your experience and qualifications, this would be a good time to go over what you consider to be your "value" in relation to the position. If the individual really pushes for a figure and you are unable to turn the question around, do some quick math and come up with a salary range that is twenty to thirty percent above your current salary. For example, if you are making $50,000 a year at present, your salary requirement should be *"in the $60,000 to $70,000 range."* But be realistic. Your information gathering should have prepared you with salary data for your geographic area.

91. **Always be prepared to ask questions during a telephone screening interview.** Candidates that often impress employers the most are ones who ask thoughtful questions about the job and organization. The ability to ask thoughtful questions indicates a certain degree of interest, initiative, and intelligence on your part.

92. **Outline the questions you need to ask for all types of telephone calls.** Whether your are making cold or referral calls to uncover job information, advice, and referrals or anticipating a telephone screening interview, it's always best to keep near your a list of questions you want to ask. In fact, it's okay to take a short list of questions with you to the face-to-face interview. It is preferable to integrate these questions throughout your telephone conversation. However, if you have been unable to cover them during the conversation, you can wait until the end and include them as a separate topic. Preface this question section with the following statement:

    "I have a few additional questions I would like to ask you. Do you have a few more minutes?"

    Then ask your questions, summarize your conversation, and use an appropriate close. In your follow-up thank you note you might want to reiterate a few of your most important questions.

Answers and Responses

93. **Keep your answers short and focused on the point.** Avoid giving answers that are too short or too long. Most responses to

questions should take 20 to 90 seconds. Shorter answers may communicate that you lack both interest and substance. Longer answers may indicate you talk too much! Both are deadly sins in the job search. Keep your answers focused on the point. Individuals who give lengthy answers to questions often drone on and on. They frequently wander off the point and talk about subjects other than those ostensibly under discussion. Shorter answers help keep you focused on the point.

94. **Avoid repeating the same answer to different questions.** Redundancy has a place in the job search, but be careful that you don't repeat yourself too often over the phone. Focus on four or five main points that stress your value to potential employers.

Positive Content

95. **Use positive content when answering questions.** Many people have a bad habit of using negative terms. Always try to answer questions in a positive, upbeat manner. This means using positive rather than negative language. Avoid negative terms, such as *"can't," "didn't,"* or *"wouldn't."* For example, instead of saying *"I don't like to travel on weekends,"* say *"I prefer traveling during the week."* Instead of saying *"I left my last job because of the low pay and long hours,"* say *"I left my last job because I wanted to seek new opportunities."* Employers tend to be attracted to individuals who use positive language.

Positive Form

96. **Use positive form when phrasing questions and answers.** What you want to achieve is positive form. This means avoiding negatives by presenting yourself in as positive a light as possible. For example, if during a telephone screening interview you have an opportunity to discuss a position, you might do the following: rather than ask *"What are the duties of _____ position?"*, ask *"What would be my duties?"* This form of questioning subtly plants the positive thought of you in the position.

Follow-Up

97. **You must follow-up your calls as well as follow-up your follow-up calls.** Follow-up is the key to turning contacts into job interviews and offers. Unfortunately, many job seekers are good at making initial contacts but they fail to follow-up. You must make a concerted effort to constantly follow-up your tele-search activities with more phone calls and letters. Persistence in following up job leads will be rewarded with job interviews and offers.

Recordkeeping

98. **Keep good records of all your tele-search activities.** You should maintain both a calendar and file of your tele-search activities. Once you launch your tele-search activities, you may be making dozens, if not hundreds, of calls. If you don't maintain a good recordkeeping system, your tele-search activities may quickly get out of hand. You'll have difficulty remembering whom you called, you may confuse the people you talked with, and you may make embarrassing mistakes when individuals return your calls.

Pagers

99. **If you are difficult to contact by telephone, you may want to use a pager.** Pagers are an increasingly popular and inexpensive way to track and screen important calls. If you use a pager, include the number in your communication with others.

Faxes

100. **Be prepared to both send and receive faxes during your job search.** More and more employers request copies of resumes and supporting documents by fax. If you don't have a fax machine, make sure you know where you can get quick access to a fax. If you use a computer, you may have a fax option available on your wordprocessing program or you can purchase inexpensive fax software. Many quick copy and business supply

stores offer fax services. Check out the ones nearest you so you are prepared to quickly receive and send faxes.

101. **Your fax cover sheet should look professional and include all the necessary contact information.** Be sure to include a fax cover sheet with your transmission. Avoid using cutesy or cartoon fax cover sheets. The basic fax cover sheet should include your name, address, telephone and fax numbers, and the transmission time. If you use a computer, check for a fax template in your word processing program. Programs such as WordPerfect 6.1 include standard fax cover sheets that look very professional and are easy to complete.

Electronic Communication Systems

102. **Explore the Internet and various commercial electronic communication systems for job information and leads.** Electronic communication is the new frontier for job seekers. The Internet and various commercial electronic communication systems, such as America Online, BIX, CompuService, Prodigy, Delphi, or GEnie, open new opportunities to engage in electronic networking via your telephone and computer. Using a telephone modem in conjunction with a computer and appropriate software, you can use the Internet to gather job information, engage in discussion groups, and identify job opportunities. This information highway literally opens you to a global communication network full of surprising information which may turn into useful job contacts. Most of the commercial electronic communication systems include a career center where you can exchange job information, review job listings, and upload your resume. For more information on how to use your telephone and computer together in today's new information highway, see the following books:

Kennedy, Joyce Lain, *Hook Up, Get Hired* (New York: Wiley, 1995)

Kennedy, Joyce Lain and Thomas J. Morrow, *Electronic Job Search Revolution* (New York: Wiley, 1994)

Dixon, Pam and Sylvia Tiersten, *Be Your Own Headhunter: Go Online to Get the Job You Want* (New York: Random House Electronic, 1995)

Jandt, Fred E. and Mary Nemnick, *Using the Internet in Your Job Search* (Indianapolis, IN: JIST Works, Inc. 1995)

Gonyea, James C., *The On-Line Job Search Companion* (New York: McGraw-Hill, 1995)

Most of these books are available directly from Impact Publications (see the order form at the end of this book).

Job Hotlines

103. Incorporate appropriate job hotlines in your tele-search campaign. More and more organizations in both the public and private sectors routinely list job openings and vacancy information on pre-recorded job hotlines. Many of these hotlines have 800 numbers. You may want to call several of these hotlines to find out if they have job openings appropriate for your interests, skills, and experience. See Chapter 5 for information on these hotlines.

4

DISCOVER JOBS ON THE INFORMATION HIGHWAY

*Y*ou can link your job search campaign to today's exploding information highway via your telephone line. Indeed, there's an electronic revolution taking place in the employment field. It centers on using computer modems to log on to databases via telephone lines. This revolution is changing the way people find jobs and how employers conduct the hiring process. You would be wise to understand this revolution. For you may want to join it today as well as participate in it for many years to come.

79

WELCOME TO THE REVOLUTION

The way people go about finding jobs—responding to classified ads, networking, using employment firms, executive search firms or headhunters, and career counselors—has not changed greatly during the past fifty years. The same is true for how employers go about locating candidates and hiring—networking, placing classified ads, and using employment firms and headhunters. In such a system, job hunters and employers come together in a highly decentralized and fragmented job market characterized by poor communication, intrigue, uncertainty, numerous rejections, high levels of anxiety, and random luck. While no one really likes this system, no one has developed a better system to link talented individuals to vacant positions—at least not until now. In the meantime, individuals learn entrepreneurial strategies, such as tele-search, for operating within this less than perfect system.

The electronic communication revolution has the potential to significantly change job search and hiring approaches. It may eliminate much of the decentralization, fragmentation, uncertainty, chaos, and anxiety in the hiring process. Most important of all, it promises to dramatically improve communication between employers and job seekers and, in the process, redefine the structure and coherence of the job market.

OLD DREAMS, NEW UTOPIAS

Employment specialists have long dreamed of creating a nationwide computerized information highway for employment. Ideally, a computerized job bank would list all available job vacancies throughout the nation. Job seekers and employers could use such a system to quickly develop linkages to each other through an efficient and effective electronic network system. No longer would employers need to engage in a costly and time consuming process of placing classified ads or hiring employment firms to find needed personnel. Job seekers would be able to quickly identify vacancies for which they are most qualified. They could eliminate the time consuming and frustrating process of responding to classified ads, broadcasting resumes and letters, networking, and literally knocking on doors. So goes the dream.

The job search revolution taking place today is not exactly what employment specialists have long envisioned. While many state employment offices, libraries, and educational institutions have computerized job banks on-line, such as America's Job Bank, most of these systems are limited in scope, include only certain types of jobs, and focus on a few geographic areas. They are by no means at the forefront of the much touted "national information highway" of the future. No comprehensive, nationwide computerized job bank has yet been created to centralize job vacancy information and thereby create a truly national job market. In the meantime, the job market remains decentralized, fragmented, and chaotic. Success in this market primarily requires formal application and interpersonal strategies for linking individual qualifications to employer needs.

Nonetheless, signs of a job search/hiring revolution are readily apparent for the 1990s and into the 21st century. It's taking on a new and unexpected form. Using computer technology to link job seekers to employers, this revolution is organized and directed by a few innovative computerized job bank firms that use sophisticated search and retrieval software that quickly links employers to job seekers. Employers and individuals become members, paying yearly or per search fees to participate in the database. The key to making the system work efficiently and effectively is for a large number of both employers and job seekers to belong to the database. The larger the number of members and the broader the mix of skills and opportunities, the better the choices for all members involved.

This revolution is an efficient way of linking employers to candidates.

In its simplest form, this revolution is an efficient way of linking employers to candidates. For you the job seeker, it's a high-tech way of broadcasting your resume to hundreds of employers. Within the next ten years electronic networks will transform the way job seekers market themselves to potential employers. Working from their personal computers, or through computerized job search services with extensive electronic resume and employer banks, job seekers will be able to quickly broadcast their qualifications to thousands of employers. No longer will they need to spend three, six, or nine months pounding the pavement, responding to classified job ads, attending meetings, making cold telephone calls, contacting strangers, or scheduling informational interviews. Indeed, many of the traditional job search methods outlined in this book may well become obsolete in this new electronic employment era. At least these appear to be the promises of the electronic revolution for the job markets of tomorrow.

Since electronic job search methods are likely to cut job search time by 50 to 70 percent, they should prove to be a cost effective way of linking candidates to employers. Employers will find they cost less and may generate better quality candidates than their more traditional recruitment methods of placing classified ads, hiring employment firms, or broadcasting vacancy announcements. Job seekers will discover that electronic networking enables them to reach a very broad sample of employers that would not be available through other job search methods.

Offering new job search and hiring options for individuals and employers alike, electronic job search services have quickly become one of the most efficient and effective ways of matching qualified candidates to employers. It will displace many current inefficient and ineffective employment services. It drastically improves communication as well as creates a certain degree of centralization in what is inherently a decentralized job market.

But that is just part of the story, the most visible part most people understand. So far computer technology has been used to make a traditional process more efficient—improve communication between job seekers and employers. The next stage is now evolving as the technology is literally redefining the process. The really revolutionary dimension of these electronic job banks is their potential to significantly alter the way people view their careers, conduct a job search, and hire.

The concept of "career fitness" explains what may well become a normal way of managing your career in the future. It's a concept worth understanding and exploring.

CAREER FITNESS IN
THE ELECTRONIC AGE

"Career fitness" is an obvious health analogy adapted to the career field. Emphasizing development and growth, this concept implies keeping your career healthy not just today or tomorrow but throughout your worklife. As enunciated by Peter Weddle, CEO of Job Bank USA, it's a lifelong concept of how you go about managing your career. Rather than initiate a job search only when you lose your job or become dissatisfied with your work—the career crisis approach—you should constantly manage your career by keeping yourself marketable and available for alternative opportunities. You can easily do this by becoming a member of one or more electronic job banks where you can literally be in the job market 24 hours a day, 7 days a weeks, and 365 days a year. Your membership does not mean you are actively seeking employment; rather, you are constantly keeping yourself marketable or "fit" for new and exciting opportunities that may come your way because you keep an updated resume in the database. While you work, your resume is always working for you. Your electronic resume is the key element for defining and directing your career fitness. As envisioned by "career fitness" advocates, individuals should seriously consider becoming lifelong members of such groups, regardless of whether or not they are actively seeking new employment.

You can literally be in the job market 24 hours a day, 7 days a week, and 365 days a year.

THE NEW ELECTRONIC RESUME

Computerized job banks use electronic resumes for linking candidates to employers. While similar in many ways to traditional resumes, the electronic resume is different. It requires close attention to the choice of resume **language** because your resume must be "read" by search and retrieval software. The software literally takes key words identified in employers' vacancy announcements and matches them with similar key words found on resumes. If, for example, an employer is looking for a human resources manager with ten years of progressive experience in developing training programs for mining engineers, a search for candidates meeting these qualifications may result in making matches with 15 resumes in the database. The employer receives hard copies of the electronic resumes and further sorts the batch of candidates through more traditional means such as telephone screening interviews.

These new electronic job search and hiring systems have important implications for resume writing. When you write an electronic resume, you must focus on using **proper resume language** that would be most responsive for the search and retrieval software. This means knowing what key words are best to include on an electronic resume. You also still need to be concerned with such cosmetic elements as resume layout, type faces, and paper texture and color. These "dressed for success" elements, though not important to the search and retrieval software of electronic job banks, are important once your resume is selected since many firms will send a hard copy of your resume to the potential employer. Therefore, you will need to write a different type of resume for your "career fitness."

MEET THE NEW
GENERATION OF PLAYERS

During the past few years numerous firms have gotten into the electronic resume business. Many of them use electronic e-mail communications, on-line bulletin boards, and existing nationwide on-line computer networks such as America Online, CompuServe, and Prodigy. Primarily funded by large Fortune 1,000 corporations, these electronic employment data-based companies include as members individuals, professional associations, and alumni, retirement, military, and other groups who are interested in linking electronic resumes to member companies. These electronic resume services become new employer-employee networks which are redefining the job market-place. The marketplace is no longer confined to the classified ads, employment firms, or executive search firms. These firms may bring together over 100,000 members into an electronic network which is constantly seeking to find "good fits" between the needs of employers and the key words appearing on members' electronic resumes.

Several electronic job banks offer these unique resume and job search services. The major firms include the following:

JOB BANK USA: 1420 Spring Hill Road, Suite 480, McLean, VA 22102, Tel. 800-296-1USA or Fax 703-847-1494. Advertised as "the nation's premier database company," Job Bank USA is an all purpose employment resource for both employers and job seekers. More than 35 educational institutions participate, including the University of Notre Dame, Fairleigh Dickinson University, The American University, University of California (Irvine), the University of Texas (Arlington), the University of Arkansas, the University of Maryland, the United States Military Academy, and the University of Louisville. Graduating seniors and alumni associated with these institutions give employers access to a growing pool of degreed professionals, from entry-level to senior executive. Individuals can enroll in the Job Bank USA database for a basic annual fee of $48.50. Other levels of enrollment cost $78.00 and $129.00. Enrollment includes:

- Conversion of your work experience and employment credentials into a unique electronic resume.

- Storage of your electronic resume in Job Bank USA's computer for one year.

- Access to a toll free telephone number to make a reasonable number of updates and corrections to your electronic resume.

- Exclusive discounts on a wide range of career management and job search services, books, and other resources.

- Unlimited referral to Job Bank USA clients who have open positions for which you qualify.

- A quarterly newsletter—*CAREERPLUS*—published exclusively for database enrollees. Includes important job market observations as well as useful ideas and tips for job seekers.

Guaranteeing privacy, Job Bank USA only releases your resume to prospective employers with your prior approval. Job Bank USA also offers testing/assessment and resume writing services. Its executive search service is aimed at linking high quality candidates to employers. This service normally deals with positions offering a base salary of $100,000 or more.

CONNEXION®: Peterson's Connexion® Services, 202 Carnegie Center, P.O. Box 2123, Princeton, NJ 08543-2123, Tel. 800-338-3282, Ext. 561 or Fax 609-243-9150. Advertised as "the innovative recruitment network that links you with thousands of employers and graduate schools who may be seeking candidates with your specific experience or training." Unlike other electronic networks, Connexion® includes graduate schools in its recruitment base. Membership is free for currently enrolled full-time students. Other individuals can enroll for an annual fee of $40. Individuals who do not want their resumes sent to employers, but who want access to other Connexion® privileges and communiques, can join as Associate Members for an annual fee of $24.95. This network can be accessed on CompuServe.

CAREER PLACEMENT REGISTRY: Career Placement Registry, Inc., 302 Swann Ave., Alexandria, VA 22301, Tel. 800-368-3093 or 703-683-1085. Includes over 110,000 employers in its database. Individuals can register for a six month period for a variety of fees, depending on desired salary level. For example, students can register for $15; individuals seeking a job up to $20,000 register for $25; those with salary expectations in the $20,000-$40,000 range register for $35; those expecting a $40,000+ salary register for $45. Recruiters can access the Career Placement Registry on DIALOG.

CAREER NET ONLINE: 1788 Wyrick Avenue, San Jose, CA 95124, Tel. 800-392-7967. Includes over 900 employers but reports only 3,000 resumes in database. Costs $42 a year to register. Individuals complete a file questionnaire.

E-SPAN JOB SEARCH: 8440 Woodfield Crossing, Suite 170, Indianapolis, IN 46240, Tel. 800-682-2901. Free service. Includes between 100 and 150 employers along with 3,500 job seekers. Individuals submit resumes through e-mail on the Internet or through CompuServe.

SKILLSEARCH: 3354 Perimeter Hill Dr., Suite 235, Nashville, TN 37211, Tel. 800-258-6641. Includes 500 employers and 35,000 candidates. Costs $65 for two years with a $15 annual renewal fee. Individuals must have a college degree plus two years of work experience. Members can initiate unlimited updates to their resume as well as receive a quarterly newsletter. Over 60 alumni associations participate in this database.

AMERICAN COMPUTERIZED EMPLOYMENT SERVICE (ACES): P.O. Box 27907, Santa Ana, CA 92799-7907, Tel. 714-434-1294. Includes more than 100 employers and 7,000 candidates. Costs $49.95 a year. Membership is open to anyone. Primarily focuses on the Southern California market.

DATAMATION DATABANK: 265 S. Main St., Akron, OH 44308, Tel. 800-860-2252. Includes 700 employers and 200,000 candidates. Primarily designed for experienced engineers and data-processing professionals, although membership is open to other individuals.

UNIVERSITY PRONET: 3803 E. Bayshore Dr., Suite 150, Palo Alto, CA 94303, Tel. 415/691-1600. Includes 250 employers and 50,000 candidates. Costs $35 for a lifetime membership. Only graduates of participating colleges and universities can participate. Includes such institutions as the University of California (Los Angeles and Berkeley), University of Chicago, Columbia University, Cornell University, University of Michigan, MIT, Stanford University, University of Wisconsin at Madison, Yale University).

INTERNET: Online Career Center, Online Resume Service, 1713 Hemlock Lane, Plainfield, IN 46168. This nonprofit organization, sponsored by 40 major corporations, allows job seekers to review hundreds of vacancy announcements posted in its computer database. It also accepts resumes so that companies can search for talented employees. For a fee of only $10.00, job seekers can have their resume entered into the computer database for a 90 day period. Computer users can browse through hundreds of vacancy announcements and resumes by accessing Internet, a worldwide group of 11,000 public and private computer networks used by nearly 10 million people. Approximately 3,000 companies use Internet for recruiting purposes. The key to accessing the Online Career Center database to use this system is having access to Internet. Those with such access should send an electronic mail message to: occmsen.com and type "info" on the subject line. You will receive instructions on what to do next. If you do not yet have access to Internet—but you do have a computer and modem—you can gain access to Internet by contacting the following companies: America Online (800-827-6364); CompuServe (800-848-8199); Delphi (800-491-3393); IDS (401-884-7856); or Worldline (800-NET-2-YOU). Finally, if you do not have a computer and modem, send a copy of your resume along with $6.00 to: Online Resume Service, 1713 Hemlock Lane, Plainfield, IN 46168. If your resume runs more than three pages, add $1.50 for each additional page. Your resume will be entered in the database for 90 days. Our advice: now may be the time to acquire that computer and modem you have been putting off for so long! For less than $1,000 you can be fully equipped to use such an electronic job network 24 hours a day, 7 days a week, and 365 days a year. Finding a good job with the assistance of a computer could more than pay for the cost of equipment. But make this purchase only if you can afford it. You should justify its use for other job search activities, such as producing resumes, writing letters, and organizing job search activities. It also should improve your overall computer literacy.

For a broad offering of nationwide job vacancies, contact the following organization:

ADNET ONLINE
ADNET Employment Advertising Network
5987 E. 71 St., Suite 206
Indianapolis, IN 46220
Tel. 800-543-9974 or 317-579-6922

Adnet Online claims to have nearly 1.5 million resumes in their system. This network can be accessed on Prodigy.

Several other electronic networks may also prove useful for your job search. If, for example, you are separating from the military, you should definitely contact the following organizations which provide career transition services:

DORS (Defense Outplacement Referral System)
ATTN: Operation Transition
99 Pacific St., Suite 155A
Monterey, CA 93940-2453
Tel. 800-727-3677

TOPS: TROA's Officer Placement Service
The Retired Officers Association
201 N. Washington St.
Alexandria, VA 22314
Tel. 800-245-8762 or 703-549-2311

Veterans Employment Assistance (VEA) Program
Non Commissioned Officers Association
10635 IH 35 North
San Antonio, TX 78233
Tel. 210-653-6161

Each of these organizations operates resume databases for matching candidates with employers. Using a standardized form, participants complete mini-resumes which are scanned into electronic resume databases. Most of these programs are open to active duty personnel and their spouses. Some also are open to veterans, reservists, and National Guard members. You should contact each of the organizations for information on their specific services.

For individuals interested in human resources positions, contact the following organization:

HUMAN RESOURCE INFORMATION NETWORK
9585 Valparaiso Ct.
Indianapolis, IN 46268
Tel. 800-421-8884 or 317-872-2045

If you are interested in manufacturing, engineering, or computer positions, contact the following job-matching resume database ($19.95 for 3 months):

CAREERS ONLINE
710 Fehr Road
Louisville, KY 40206
Tel. 502-894-9887

You might also consider the employment networking potential of the three major telecommunication services which operate as electronic bulletin boards. Each includes a "career corner" of job vacancies and career services:

AMERICA ONLINE
8619 Westwood Center Dr.
Vienna, VA 22182
Tel. 800-827-6364

COMPUSERVE
CompuService Information Service
5000 Arlington Centre Boulevard
Columbus, OH 43220
Tel. 800-848-8199

PRODIGY
Prodigy Services Company
445 Hamilton Avenue
White Plains, NY 10601
Tel. 800-776-3449 or 914-993-8000

You will need a personal computer, telephone modem, and communications software to interact with these services. Chances are you will electronically meet new people and organizations that can provide job leads for someone with your interests and qualifications.

American Online (AOL) operates one of the largest and most comprehensive career centers. Using a personal computer and telephone modem, you can access AOL's Career Center where you will discover several useful career services: articles, career counselors, resource library, resumes and cover letters, employer databases, executive search firms, educational resources, job listings, occupational profiles, and a talent bank. For more information, call AOL at 1-800-827-6364 or get a copy of James Gonyea's book, *The On-Line Job Search Companion* (see below), which includes a disk to access America Online.

KEY ELECTRONIC NETWORKING RESOURCES

A few new books provide useful information on the new electronic job search and hiring era. The major such resources include the following books:

Dixon, Pam and Sylvia Tiersten, *Be Your Own Headhunter: Go Online to Get the Job You Want* (New York: Random House Electronic, 1995)

Gonyea, James C., *The On-Line Job Search Companion* (New York: McGraw-Hill, 1995). Includes a free copy of a computer disk to access America Online's Career Center.

Kennedy, Joyce Lain, *Hook Up, Get Hired* (New York: Wiley, 1995)

Kennedy, Joyce Lain and Thomas J. Morrow, *Electronic Job Search Revolution* (New York: Wiley, 1994)

Kennedy, Joyce Lain and Thomas J. Morrow, *Electronic Resume Revolution* (New York: Wiley, 1994)

Jandt, Fred E. and Mary Nemnick, *Using the Internet in Your Job Search* (Indianapolis, IN: JIST Works, Inc., 1995)

Weddle, Peter D., *Electronic Resumes for the New Job Market: Resumes That Work for You 24 Hours a Day* (Manassas Park, VA: Impact Publications, 1995)

During the next ten years we expect an explosion of new electronic job search and hiring services—from electronic resume banks and on-line job vacancy bulletin boards to CD-ROM programs for developing new forms of job search communication. Right now these services are in their infancy, primarily used by individuals with high-tech skills, and confined to a group of 3-5 million computer users. While you may encounter a chaotic and bewildering array of such services, each competing for more and more database enrollees, one thing is certain: electronic job search and hiring services are here to stay. Employers will use these services more and more because they offer efficient and effective ways of tapping into nationwide talent pools. Job seekers will increasingly use the services because they can reach many more employers electronically than they could through more traditional direct-mail and networking methods.

BEWARE OF THE LAZY WAY TO SUCCESS

While electronic job search services may well be the wave of the future, they will by no means displace the more traditional job search methods outlined in previous chapters of this book. Indeed, there is a danger in thinking that the electronic revolution will offer **the** solution to the inefficiencies and ineffectiveness associated with traditional job search methods. As presently practiced, electronic networking is primarily a method for disseminating resumes to potential employers who wish to hire individuals with high-tech skills. As such, it is a high-tech vacancy announcement and resume broadcasting method. This revolution will most likely move to other levels, especially multi-media communication forms, which integrate resumes with video presentations of candidates' qualifications.

The problems with present forms of electronic networking are fourfold. First, these networks are primarily designed for and controlled by employers. Indeed, they are mostly funded by employers who have on-line access to participants' resume data. Job seekers become relatively passive participants who submit an electronic resume and then wait to hear from employers who may or may not access their resume. Not surprising, many job seekers may never hear from employers. From the perspective of the job seeker, such a network is merely a high-tech version of the broadcast resume that is mass mailed to numerous employers—one of the most ineffective resume distribution approaches.

Second, electronic resume services give employers limited, albeit important, information on candidates. These services are primarily efficient resume screening techniques that communicate little information about the individual beyond traditional resume categories. Employers still need to screen candidates on other criteria, especially in face-to-face settings, which enable them to access a candidate's personal chemistry. Such information is best communicated through the networking process.

Third, the major sponsors and participants—large Fortune 1000 companies—in the electronic resume banks are not the ones that do most of the hiring. These are the same companies that have been shedding jobs—more than 3 million in the past five years—rather than adding them to the job market. What hiring these companies do is largely for hard to find, highly skilled individuals. Most small companies—those that generate the most jobs—do not participate in these electronic job search and hiring networks. Therefore, you are well advised to target your job search toward the companies that generate the most jobs. You do so by using the major networking techniques outlined earlier in this book. If you decide to participate in an electronic job bank, do so only as a supplement to your other job search activities.

Fourth, like many predictions of futurists, the electronic job search revolution is often overstated and highly overrated. It tends to disproportionately appeal to people who prefer quick and easy approaches to the job search. They often look for the "magic pill" for job search success—one that involves the least amount of time and effort and few interpersonal contacts with potential employers. Research, networking, informational interviews, and cold calling techniques involve a great deal of interpersonal skill and have unpredictable outcomes. On the other hand, computers, modems, and electronics give many people—especially men—a false sense of making progress in what is inherently a difficult and highly ego-involved process—communicating your qualifications to strangers who are likely to reject you.

We recommend that you include electronic job search services in your overall repertoire of job search methods. But put this electronic networking alternative in its proper perspective—it's an efficient way to broadcast your qualifications to employers through an electronic resume. Don't approach electronic networking as the easy way to job search success; there's nothing magical about this resume dissemination method. Sending a $10, $20, $30, $50, or $100 membership fee and a resume to one of these firms ensures you nothing other than a presence in an electronic resume bank. What happens next—whether or not you are contacted by employers—depends on an unpredictable mix of factors, such as the number and quality of employer members in the system, employer hiring needs at any specific time, and the quality of your electronic resume, especially your choice of resume language.

THERE'S MORE TO COME

Much of our information on the electronic job search revolution will quickly become obsolete as numerous organizations continue to develop innovative electronic employment networks. Many of the current major players, such as America Online, will face intense competition from newer players on the free Internet. Indeed, keep a close eye on new job and career services appearing on the Internet. For example, Adams Media Corporation (Holbrook, MA) is launching its own online career service on the Internet in early 1995. A new online service called CareerWeb (Norfolk, VA), accessed via the World Wide Web (http://www.careerweb.com), will begin operating on the Internet by mid-1995. This well financed and innovative service has the potential to displace most other electronic job search services in the long run. Our advice: Begin navigating the information highway soon. You may be surprised what you discover on your telephone line by logging on with your computer modem!

5

DIAL JOB HOTLINES, PERSONNEL OFFICES, AND EMPLOYERS

*O*ne of the easiest ways to uncover job leads and acquire useful job information is by calling "Job Hotline" numbers. Thousands of organizations in both the public and private sectors routinely announce job vacancies on recorded telephone messages. Depending on the organization, these messages may change daily, weekly, or biweekly. If you know the right telephone number, you can monitor these vacancies and gain important job information by using your telephone.

WHAT YOU LEARN

By calling a job hotline number you can gain valuable information on employment opportunities and application procedures. Most of the recording messages include the following "Job Hotline" information:

1. Current positions open
2. Application procedures and deadlines
3. Tests and documents required

A hotline message might also announce whether or not the organization is hiring at present. In some cases the message may simply state *"We are not hiring at present."*

WHO'S WHO IN THE "HOTLINE" BUSINESS

Job hotlines are extensively used by all types of organizations. In the public sector, many personnel offices of local, state, and federal government agencies routinely operate a job hotline on which they announce job vacancies and application procedures and deadlines. Many people are unaware of this convenient service because the job hotline numbers are not widely publicized. If you want to find out if an agency has such a number, call the agency's general information number or the personnel office and ask the following question:

"Do you have a job hotline number?"

If the operator does not know, ask to speak with the personnel office. Usually the personnel office is responsible for maintaining current information on the job hotline.

Do not limit your job hotline search just to government or business organizations. Numerous professional associations and nonprofit and volunteer groups maintain placement services which include job listings and vacancy information. A good starting point for identifying many of these organizations is Dan Lauber's two books on sources of vacancy announcements, ***The Professional's Private Sector Job Finder*** and ***The Nonprofit's Job Finder***, Marcia Williams and Sue Cubbage's ***The 1995 National Job Hotline Directory,*** and Career

Communication's *Job Hotlines USA*. These books are available directly through Impact Publications (see order form at the end of this book).

PUBLIC SECTOR HOTLINES

Government agencies at the local, state, and federal levels use job hotline numbers for announcing vacancies. The messages usually include the position, grade level, application procedures, test required, and deadlines. Some will send you a copy of the vacancy announcement if you call another number and request a copy through the mail or by fax.

Please note that most government job hotlines do not include all vacant positions nor impending vacancies. Many of these hotlines only include entry-level and hard-to-fill positions, especially clerical and technical positions. You may need to visit an agency personnel office to review vacancy announcements.

Most city and county governments maintain job hotlines. For example, the following city governments in California are only a few that have job hotlines for local government positions in California:

Alameda	510/748-4635
Anaheim	714/254-5197
Bakersfield	805/326-3773
Berkeley	510/644-6122
Costa Mesa	714/754-5070
Fairfield	707/428-7396
Fullerton	714/738-6378
Los Angeles	213/485-2441
Monterey	408/646-3751
Orange	714/744-7262
Sacramento	916/443-9990
San Diego	619/236-6463
San Francisco	415/557-4888
San Jose	408/277-5627
Stockton	209/944-8523
Whittier	818/945-8226

If you are interested in a federal government job, many of the following federal agencies maintain 24-hour job hotlines. While most are found in the Washington, DC metropolitan area, many agencies in the ten federal regions also maintain personnel offices and similar hotline numbers. By calling a number, you will get a recorded message listing the latest agency vacancies as well as information on eligibility requirements and instructions for submitting an application. In most cases we have included the telephone number for the personnel office in charge of disseminating job vacancy information. In some cases, especially where several personnel offices are found within a single agency, we have included the telephone number of the director of the personnel office. You can call that number to get information on whom you should contact.

Since agencies have a habit of frequently changing their phone numbers, some of these numbers may no longer be valid. If the number has been disconnected or no new number is announced, you should contact Information for the new number. Ask for the new telephone number for the agency personnel office or the agency switch board operator. After one or two phone calls, you should be able to find the new telephone number. Ask the personnel office if they have a "Job Hotline" number you can call for current job vacancy information. Chances are they will have such a number or they have temporarily discontinued the number because the agency is not hiring at present.

FEDERAL AGENCY	Personnel Office	Job Hotline
Administrative Office of U.S. Courts	202/273-2777	202/273-2760
Agency for International Development	202/663-2396	
Agency for Toxic Substances and Disease Registry	404/639-3615	
Agriculture, Department of	202/720-5626	
Agricultural Research Service	301/344-1518	301/344-1124
		301/344-2288
Alcohol, Drug Abuse, and Mental Health Administration	301/443-4826	301/443-2282
Animal and Plant Health Inspection Service	301/734-8428	
Army Corps of Engineers	202/272-0720	
Arms Control and Disarmament Agency	202/647-2034	
Bureau of Engraving and Printing	202/874-2733	
Bureau of Indian Affairs	202/208-7581	
Bureau of Land Management	703/440-1713	
Bureau of Mines	202/501-9600	
Bureau of Public Debt	304/480-7799	
Bureau of Prisons	202/307-1304	

Bureau of Reclamation	303/236-3819	
Bureau of the Census	301/457-1722	301/457-4608
Central Intelligence Agency	703/482-0677	800/JOBSCIA
Commerce, Department of	202/482-2560	202/482-5138
		202/377-5138
Commission on Civil Rights	202/376-8364	
Commodity Futures Trading Commission	202/254-3275	
Consumer Product Safety Commission	301/504-0100	
Corporation for National and		
Community Service	202/565-5000	202/565-2800
Defense, Department of (civilian)		
▪ Air Force, Department of	703/697-9115	703/693-6550
▪ Army, Department of	703/325-8840	
▪ Consolidated Personnel Center	202/433-5370	
▪ Defense Investigative Service	703/325-6186	
▪ National Naval Medical Center	301/295-6813	
▪ Navy, Department of	703/697-6181	
▪ Walter Reed Army Medical Center	202/782-3355	
Defense Contract Audit Agency	703/274-7327	
Defense Logistics Agency	703/274-7088	
Defense Mapping Agency	703/274-7327	
District of Columbia Government	202/727-6406	202/727-9726
Drug Enforcement Administration	202/307-4055	
Education, Department of	202/401-0497	
Employment and Training		
Administration	202/219-6344	
Energy, Department of	202/586-2731	202/586-4333
Environmental Protection Agency	202/260-3144	202/260-5055
Equal Employment Opportunity		
Commission	202/663-4306	
Export-Import Bank of the U.S.	202/565-3300	
Farmers Home Administration	202/245-5561	
Federal Aviation Administration	202/267-3870	
Federal Bureau of Investigation	202/324-3674	
Federal Communications Commission	202/418-0130	
Federal Deposit Insurance Corporation	202/898-3899	
Federal Election Commission	800/424-9530	
Federal Emergency Management Agency	202/646-3964	202/646-3244
Federal Energy Regulatory		
Commission	202/219-2965	202/219-2791
Federal Housing Finance Board	202/408-2832	202/408-2517
Federal Labor Relations Authority	202/482-6660	
Federal Maritime Commission	202/523-5773	
Federal Mediation and Conciliation		
Service	202/606-5460	
Federal Reserve System	800/448-4894	202/452-3038
Federal Trade Commission	202/326-2022	

Federal Transit Administration	202/366-2513	
Financial Management Service	202/847-7080	
Food and Drug Administration	301/443-1970	301/443-1969
Food and Nutrition Service	703/305-2276	
Foreign Agricultural Service	202/720-1587	
Foreign Service	703/875-7490	
Forest Service	703/235-8102	703/235-2730
General Accounting Office	202/512-5811	202/512-6092
General Services Administration	202/501-0370	
Government Printing Office	202/512-1198	
Health and Human Services, Department of	202/619-2560	
Health Care Financing Administration	410/966-5505	
Housing and Urban Development, Department of	202/755-5395	
Immigration and Naturalization Service	202/514-2530	202/514-4301
Indian Health Service	301/443-6520	
Interior, Department of	202/208-7150	
		800/336-4562
Internal Revenue Service	202/622-6340	
International Trade Administration	202/482-3301	
International Trade Commission	202/205-2651	
Interstate Commerce Commission	202/927-7288	
Justice, Department of	202/514-6788	202/514-6818
Labor, Department of	202/219-6677	202/219-6646
Merit Systems Protection Board	202/653-5916	
National Archives & Records Administration	301/713-6760	
National Aeronautics and Space Administration	202/358-1560	
NASA Goddard Space Center	301/286-7918	301/286-5326
National Archives and Records Administration	301/713-6760	
National Capital Planning Commission	202/724-0170	
National Credit Union Administration	703/518-6510	
National Endowment for the Arts	202/682-5405	202/682-5799
National Endowment for the Humanities	202/606-8415	
National Gallery of Art	202/842-6282	202/842-6298
National Institutes of Health	301/496-2403	
National Institute of Standards and Technology	301/975-3007	301/926-4851
National Labor Relations Board	202/273-1000	
National Library of Medicine	301/496-4943	
National Oceanic and Atmospheric Administration	301/713-1377	
National Park Service	202/619-7256	301/713-0677
National Science Foundation	202/357-7602	800/628-1487

National Security Agency	800/255-8415	
National Transportation Safety Board	202/382-6717	
Naval Submarine Base (Kings Bay, GA)	912/757-3000	800/544-1707
Nuclear Regulatory Commission	301/415-7516	
Occupational Safety and Health Administration	202/219-8013	
Office of the Comptroller of the Currency	202/874-4490	
Office of Management and Budget	202/395-1088	202/395-5892
Office of Personnel Management	202/606-2424	
OPM Job Information Center		202/606-2700
Overseas Private Investment Corporation	202/663-2400	
Panama Canal Commission	202/634-6441	
Patent and Trademark Office	703/305-8231	
Peace Corps	202/606-3400	800/424-8580
Pension Benefit Guaranty Corporation	202/326-4110	
Postal Rate Commission	202/789-6840	
Postal Service	202/268-3646	202/636-1537
		800/562-8777
President, Executive Office of the	202/395-1088	
Public Health Service	301/443-6571	
Railroad Retirement Board	312/751-4579	
Securities and Exchange Commission		202/942-4150
Selective Service System	703/235-2258	
Small Business Administration	202/205-6782	
Smithsonian Institution	202/287-3100	202/287-3102
Social Security Administration	410/965-4506	
Soil Conservation Service	202/720-4264	
State, Department of	202/647-7284	
Substance Abuse and Mental Health Services Administration	301/443-5407	301/443-2282
Tennessee Valley Authority	615/632-3341	
Transportation, Department of	202/366-9394	
Treasury, Department of	202/622-1460	
U.S. Arms Control and Disarmament Agency	202/647-2034	
U.S. Coast Guard	202/267-6963	202/267-2331
U.S. Fish and Wildlife	703/358-1743	703/358-2120
U.S. Geological Survey	703/648-7442	703/648-7676
U.S. Information Agency	202/619-4659	202/619-4539
■ Bureau of Broadcasting		202/619-0909
U.S. Agency for International Development	202/647-1850	
U.S. Marshals Service	202/307-9666	
U.S. Mint	202/874-9300	415/744-9364
U.S. Secret Service	202/395-2020	

Veterans Employment and Training
   Administration   202/219-6677
Veterans Affairs, Department of   202/273-4931
Voice of America   202/619-3117

For more complete and up-to-date listing of federal personnel offices, refer to current agency telephone directories.

Congress and the legislative bureaucracy employs thousands of individuals. Most of these positions are found in Washington, DC. The following legislative agencies announce vacancies:

	Personnel Office	Job Hotline
Congressional Budget Office	202/226-2621	
General Accounting Office	202/512-5811	
Government Printing Office	202/275-2951	
Library of Congress	202/707-5627	202/707-4315
▪ Congressional Research Service	202/707-8803	
Office of Technology Assessment	202/224-8713	
U.S. Botanic Garden	202/225-1231	

If you are interested in working for the U.S. Congress as a personnel staff member or committee staff member, contact the following offices on Capitol Hill:

House Placement Office   202/226-6731
Senate Placement Office   202/224-9167

For more information on government employment, see our three books on this subject: *The Complete Guide to Public Employment*, *Find a Federal Job Fast*, and *The Directory of Federal Jobs and Employers*. We also highly recommend Dan Lauber's *The Government Job Finder* which includes telephone numbers of numerous local, state, and federal government personnel agencies, job hotlines, and public employee professional associations. All of these books are available directly from Impact Publications.

NONGOVERNMENTAL HOTLINES

Numerous professional associations, nonprofit organizations, and businesses maintain job hotlines. The following organizations, which operate at the local, state, or national levels, represent only a few of the many thousands of similar organizations that have job hotlines and encourage candidates to call them for updated vacancy information.

Alabama Gas Corporation (Birmingham)	205/326-8190
Alaska Airlines (Anchorage)	206/433-3230
Airline Pilot's Association	703/689-4262
American Association for Respiratory Disease	214/241-7249
American Library Association	800/545-2433
Association of College and Research Libraries	312/944-6795
Battelle Memorial Institute (Columbus, OH)	614/424-5627
Beech Aircraft Corporation (Wichita, KS)	316/676-8435
Career America Connection	912/757-3000
Carnival Cruise Lines (Miami)	305/471-4780
Choice International Hotels	800/348-2041
Computer Data Systems	800/772-2374
Coors Brewing Company (Golden, CO)	303/277-2450
Corporation for Public Broadcasting	202/393-1045
Discovery Network (Bethesda, MD)	301/986-0444
Employee Relocation Council	202/857-0842
Gannett Company Inc. (Arlington, VA)	703/284-6054
Land O'Lakes Inc.	612/481-2250
Levi Strauss and Company (San Francisco)	415/544-7828
MCI International	800/888-2413
Microsoft Corporation (Seattle, WA)	206/936-5500
Minnesota Mutual Life Insurance (St. Paul)	612/298-7934
Mobile Oil Corporation (Fairfax, VA)	703/846-2777
National Hospice Organization	703/243-4348
National Public Radio (Washington, DC)	202/414-3030
New York Times	212/556-1383
Nissan Motor Manufacturing Corp. (Smyrna, TN)	615/355-2243
Northern Telecome	800/667-8437
Northrop Corporation (Los Angeles)	213/600-4025
Pacificorp (Portland, OR)	503/464-6848
PetsMart	800/899-7387
St. Louis University (St. Louis, MO)	314/977-2265
San Diego National Trust & Savings Bank	619/557-2473
Shopper's Food Warehouse (Lanham, MD)	301/306-8600
Southwest Airlines (Dallas, TX)	214/904-4803
United Airlines System Jobline	708/952-7077
University of North Carolina Hospitals	919/966-1263
Vulcan Materials Company (Birmingham, AL)	205/877-3986
Walt Disney World (Lake Buena Vista, FL)	407/828-3088
Washington Post	202/334-5350

RESOURCES FOR
MAKING KEY CONTACTS

For an extensive listing of job hotlines nationwide, we recommend the following directories:

Marcia Williams and Sue Cubbage's *The 1995 National Job Hotline Directory* (New York: McGraw-Hill)

Job Hotlines USA (Harleysville, PA: Career Communications, Inc.)

These books include hundreds of job hotline numbers for all types of organizations and employers, from government and education to hospitals, hotels, and banks. However, be forwarded that telephone numbers do change and companies do move or go out of business. Indeed, some of the telephone numbers appearing in this chapter may already have changed.

Numerous other directories include contact information on thousands of potential employers. Some of these resources are organized on a state by state basis, such as Adams Media's *Denver JobBank, New York JobBank, Los Angeles JobBank, Chicago JobBank,* and *Philadelphia JobBank* and Surrey Book's *How to Get a Job in Atlanta, How to Get a Job in Washington, DC,* and *How to Get a Job in Dallas/Fort Worth.* Adams Media also produces the *National JobBank* and *America's Fastest Growing Employers.* Many of their job bank books are available through Adams Media's new on-line job service (Adams Media, 260 Center Street, Holbrook, MA 02343). The *Hoover's Handbook of America Business, Hoover's Handbook of World Business,* and *Hoover's Masterlist of 2,500 of America's Largest and Fastest Growing Employers* (Ready Reference Press), produced annually, provide a wealth of contact information on major employers. Scope International's software program, *JobHunt for Windows*™, provides contact information, including telephone and fax numbers, on 6,000 major employers; their program also allows you to develop resumes and letters targeted to the employers in their database. We especially like *The National Directory of Addresses and Telephone Numbers* (Omnigraphics) and *The Encyclopedia of Associations* (Gale Research) which are available in both paper and

CD-ROM versions. *The Job Hunter's Yellow Pages* (Career Communications) also should prove useful. Most of these resources are
available from Impact Publications.

6

SAMPLE DIALOGUES, MESSAGES & SCENARIOS

While you should never regurgitate memorized lines nor read what you want to say over the telephone, you should have a good strategy for approaching each person you wish to contact.

This chapter introduces several common tele-search dialogues, messages, and scenarios similar to those you will likely encounter throughout your job search. Each dialogue illustrates a particular tele-search situation commonly found in most job searches. Please examine each scenario for ideas in developing **your own** messages.

Keep in mind that you always want to sound interesting, intelligent, enthusiastic, and likable over the telephone. You do this in the way

106

you introduce yourself, through the common ground elements you establish, in the tone of your voice, and by the types of questions you ask. All of our examples incorporate the various tips and strategies we discussed in previous chapters.

ACQUIRING INFORMATION, ADVICE, AND REFERRALS

Many of your telephone initiatives—probably the majority—will be aimed at acquiring job information, advice, and referrals. You make these types of calls in order to build and expand your networks. Most of these calls will be made as cold or referral calls. The following examples are relatively effective cold call approaches to gathering job information, advice, and referrals:

Cold Call for Contact Information

CALLER: *"Hi. This is Terri Bays. I'm trying to contact the person in charge of marketing. Who would that be?"*

RECEIVER: *"That's Eric Walton. He's the Director."*

CALLER: *"I need to contact him about some marketing concerns. Does he have a direct number or an extension number?"*

RECEIVER: *"His number is 281-7821. Should I transfer you?"*

ANALYSIS: This is a straightforward call for information. It follows the basic *"I'm X, who's Y, and how do I reach Y?"* format. Most gatekeepers volunteer this information with no questions asked—if you mention that you have "business" to conduct.

Cold Call With Message

CALLER: *"This is Terri Bays calling for Eric Walton."*

RECEIVER: *"Mr. Walton is in a meeting at present. Would you like to leave a message?"*

CALLER: *"Yes. Could you tell him Terri Bays called. My number is 731-3000. I would like to speak with him concerning his work in . . . . I'll be in my office the rest of the day as well as between 9:00am and 4:00pm tomorrow. Thank you."*

ANALYSIS: The caller immediately identifies herself and requests to speak with the person. Given this direct *"I'm X calling for Y"* approach, the gatekeeper may assume you know the person and thus be more willing to field your call. When making such a cold call, you should leave a complete message in which you (1) state your name, (2) leave your phone number, (3) indicate the nature of your business, and (4) identify your availability during the next 24 hours for a return call. Whether or not you receive a return call depends in part on the quality of your message concerning the nature of your business. Leave enough information that will motivate the person to return your call—not too much nor too little. The same message should be left if the person is immediately reached by voice mail or the gatekeeper puts her through to a voice mailbox.

Cold Call Screened By Gatekeeper

CALLER: *"This is Terri Bays calling for Eric Walton."*

RECEIVER: *"Where are you calling from and what is the nature of your business?"*

CALLER: *"I'm calling from Indianapolis. I would like to speak with Mr. Walton about his work in . . ."*

RECEIVER: *"Let me check to see if he is available."*

Cold Call Making Direct Contact

CALLER: *"This is Terri Bays calling for Eric Walton."*

RECEIVER: *"Speaking."*

CALLER: *"I'm calling about your work in marketing. I'm in the process of gathering information on opportunities in international marketing and thought you could be a good person to talk with because of your extensive experience*

> *with Bellows International. Do you have a few minutes or would it be better if I called back at a more convenient time?"*

RECEIVER: *"I'm really not sure I can be of much help. I'm very busy right now. What type of information do you need?"*

CALLER: *"I recently completed my Bachelor's Degree in International Marketing at Indiana University. I speak Russian and have traveled extensively throughout Eastern Europe. I really want to start my career in this fascinating part of the world, but I'm not sure how to best proceed at this point. I'm now gathering information on pharmaceutical companies that have begun marketing their products in Russia and the Newly Independent States. Since I know you've done extensive international marketing, do you know who the major players are in this region? I'm trying to identify four or five of the key companies that are either currently in the area or interested in expanding their operations there."*

ANALYSIS: The caller has a nice low-keyed approach that is considerate, pleasant, and persistent. She immediately establishes common ground by linking her background to the receiver's experience. While seeking information and contacts, she clearly communicates her interest and enthusiasm by mentioning her educational background and travel experience. She invites the receiver to give her advice and thus creates the role of counselor for the receiver. She is not asking for a job—only information and advice. She'll most likely ask for referrals at the very end of this conversation. Best of all for a cold call, she sounds interesting, intelligent, and adventuresome. This is someone the receiver will probably decide to talk with for more than just a few minutes. Even though she is a stranger, he will probably like her and want to help her.

Referral With Gatekeeper

CALLER: *"Hi, this is Jim Taylor calling for Margaret Davis."*

RECEIVER: *"Miss Davis is in a meeting at present. Would you like to leave a message?"*

CALLER: *"Yes. Could you tell her Jim Taylor called. My number is 214-2790. Melissa Warner recommended that I call her about her work in . . . . I'll be in my office the rest of the day as well as between 9:00am and 4:00pm tomorrow. Thank you."*

ANALYSIS: Similar to the Terri Bays/Eric Walton cold call, the caller in this case immediately identifies himself and requests to speak with the person—the direct *"I'm X calling for Y"* approach. The gatekeeper will probably assume the caller knows the person. When the caller learns the person is not available, he leaves a message mentioning his referral contact. He has a high probability of getting a return call. He should leave the same message if he immediately encounters voice mail or the gatekeeper puts him through to a voice mailbox.

Referral Direct

CALLER: *"This is Terri Bays calling for Eric Walton."*

RECEIVER: *"Speaking."*

CALLER: *"John Pinkerton recommended that I call about your work in marketing."*

RECEIVER: *"How is John? I haven't spoken with him for some time."*

CALLER: *"John's doing great. He just returned from a two-month research project in the Ukraine. He's doing some fascinating work on a pilot agricultural marketing project sponsored by the UN. In fact, he recommended that I call you because you taught together in the Marketing Department at Michigan State University several years ago. He spoke very highly of you."*

RECEIVER: *"That's great to hear. John's always doing interesting and innovative work. Please give him my regards. So, how can I help you?"*

CALLER: *"I recently completed my Bachelor's Degree in International Marketing at Indiana University. I speak Russian and have traveled extensively . . . "*

ANALYSIS: This is the most effective type of tele-search call you can make. It helps you quickly develop and expand your job search network. The caller already has a personal contact for establishing common ground. In contrast to other types of calls, referral calls often begin with a few moments of small talk. This type of small talk helps transfer the personal relationship existing between your referral and the receiver to you. It helps develop a cooperative relationship that should result in greater depth of information, advice, and referrals.

FOLLOW UPS

You need to make several types of follow-up calls throughout your job search. Failure to follow-up is one of the major reasons many job seekers have difficulty making progress in the job market. You simply must follow-up often and do so by telephone. The following are the most frequent type of follow-up calls you need to make.

Thank You

CALLER: *"Hi, this is Jerry Winton calling for Jonathan Arthur."*

RECEIVER: *"Speaking."*

CALLER: *"Thanks so much for referring me to Jill Balinger last week. You were right. She really knows the leasing business, and I'm most impressed with the work she is doing in marine leasing. We had a wonderful talk this morning and she invited me to meet with her next Tuesday about a position with her firm. I just wanted to let you know how much I appreciated your advice and reference. I'll let you know the outcome."*

ANALYSIS: Not only is such a thank you call a thoughtful thing to do, it also may be a wise action at this time. Because Jerry called, Jonathan may next call his contact and put in a good word for Jerry's impending candidacy. After all, Jonathan was sufficiently impressed with Jerry to give him the referral to Jill in the first place. This thank you call confirms Jonathan's wisdom for having referred Jerry to Jill. Similar types of thank you calls are appropriate for other job search occasions, such as thanking someone for useful information and advice. Perhaps someone loaned you a book or counseled you about your job search. Make a thank you follow-up call expressing your appreciation.

Resume or Application

CALLER: *"Hi, this is JoAnna Salem calling in reference to a letter and resume I sent to your office last week for the graphic design position you advertised in the Times. I wanted to check if you received it and if you had any questions."*

RECEIVER: *"Yes, we did get your resume. We're currently reviewing applications. I don't think we have any questions at this time. We'll give you a call if we do."*

CALLER: *"Do you know when you might be making the final decisions?"*

RECEIVER: *"We're trying to complete our review this week. We'll probably start interviewing sometime next week or the week after. I know Mr. Davis wants to get the position filled as soon as possible."*

CALLER: *"I'm really interested in the position. It's a perfect fit with my five years of experience in the publishing industry. Do let me know if you need any additional information. I would be happy to have you talk with several of my clients who know my work well."*

ANALYSIS: While this follow-up call yields some useful information about the decision-making process, it also may give your application added attention. The fact that the receiver had to check to see if they received your resume may help give your resume this attention. And it doesn't hurt to pitch yourself some more for the position. If you sound really good over the phone, the person may move you from the bottom of the pile to the top. You, in effect, conducted a screening interview for the position before being called by the employer for such an interview. This critical call may result in you being remembered more than other candidates. It's important that you not be too pushy when making such a call. You can easily turn off an employer by being too aggressive when making such a follow-up call. You don't want to get remembered as a jerk! Get the information, make your point, and get remembered as a professional person who can communicate well with others.

Interview

CALLER: *"Hi, this is April Sellers. I wanted to thank you again for inviting me to meet with you and your staff yesterday. I want to express again my interest in the editing position. I believe my five years of editing experience and work in magazine publishing are ideally suited for this position. I was especially impressed with the quality of your publications and your talented staff. I believe we would work well together."*

RECEIVER: *"We appreciated your frank discussion of our publications. Perhaps we will have some good news for you by next week."*

CALLER: *"I'll give you a call next Tuesday. Since your position is my first choice, I want to hear from you before making any other decisions. Do let me know if you have any other questions."*

ANALYSIS: The caller does four things few interviewees ever do in the post-interview period: (1) she expresses her gratitude, (2) she reiterates her interest in the position, (3) she indicates this employer is her number one choice, and (4) she makes an appointment for a second telephone follow-up call. Such a call often impresses an employer so much that, all other things being equal among finalists, they will hire her because of this follow-up call. Employers like to be wanted by employees. The caller expresses in the follow-up call some of the most sought-after characteristics amongst job candidates— thoughtfulness, likability, and initiative. The receiver will remember her until the final hiring decision is made. Indeed, the receiver knows she must be prepared to talk to her again on Tuesday about this position. Wouldn't it be nice to give her good news rather than deliver bad news?

Hiring Decision

CALLER: *"Hi, this is Mike Martin calling. I interviewed for the computer programmer position last week. I'm just checking to see if you have made a hiring decision?"*

RECEIVER: *"Not yet Mike. We anticipate making our final selection this Friday."*

CALLER: *"I'm still very interested in this position. You're doing some very innovative multimedia work that's on the cutting edge of today's new technology. Best of all, you have a very bright and energetic technical staff that understands the importance of team production. I'm sure we would work well together. Would it be okay if I called you on Friday? What would be the best time?"*

ANALYSIS: The caller set the stage for this type of follow-up call. He did so when closing the face-to-face interview by asking the interviewer if it would be okay to call her if he had not heard from her by Tuesday. She said that would be fine. So now he calls on Tuesday to ask about the status of the hiring decision. In the process of doing so he reiterates his interest in the position and schedules another call. This call may affect the final hiring decision in the favor of the caller—the receiver is impressed by the caller's interest in the position—he's remembered again at this critical decision-making stage. In other words, the caller really wants to work for them—an important characteristic not apparent from other candidates who failed to make such a follow-up call.

Job Offer

CALLER: *"Hi, this is Paul Miller. I wanted to thank you and your staff again for the opportunity to join your organization. I appreciate the confidence you've placed in me and promise you nothing less than 100 percent. I appreciated the professional manner in which the interviews were conducted. I was very impressed with your staff. I'm looking forward to working closely with you and your staff in the months ahead. Do let me know if there is anything I need to do between now and when I start on May 10th. For*

example, should I be in contact with the personnel depart-
ment to complete payroll and insurance information before
the 10th?"

ANALYSIS: This type of follow-up call helps set the stage for developing positive on-the-job relations. How an individual interviews and follows up often says a lot about how the person will do on the job. You communicate your thoughtfulness and likability when you make such a call. This thank you follow-up call after receiving the job offer helps confirm in the mind of those who made the hiring decision that indeed they made the right decision. You should also follow-up this call with a written thank you letter.

UNCOVERING JOB LEADS

Many people use the telephone to randomly uncover job leads. In fact, one approach of job clubs is to use the Yellow Pages to call employers directly to find out if they have vacancies. This type of call basically asks *"Do you have a job for me?"* It's the type of call that results in numerous rejections because (1) most employers contacted do not have vacancies at that particular moment and (2) employers are not keen about broadcasting vacancies to cold callers. Nonetheless, if you don't mind encountering numerous rejections and you are prepared to play the probability game, go ahead and try your luck. You might uncover two appropriate vacancies for every 100 cold calls you make. Your call might go something like this:

CALLER: *"Hi, this is Marcia Voris calling. Do you have any vacancies for word processors?"*

RECEIVER: *"Not at present."*

CALLER: *"Are you accepting applications?"*

RECEIVER: *"You can send us a resume if you wish. We'll keep it on file in case a vacancy would arise at another time. We do periodically hire for such positions."*

CALLER: *"To whom should I address my correspondence?"*

RECEIVER: *"Just send it to the Personnel Department."*

CALLER: *"I would really like to address it to a person."*

RECEIVER: *"It really doesn't matter, but go ahead and send it to Richard Merit who handles our resume bank."*

CALLER: *"Thank you very much for your assistance. By the way, what is your name?"*

RECEIVER: *"Jeffrey Plant. I'm Mr. Merit's assistant."*

ANALYSIS: While we don't put much stock in making these types of cold calls, nonetheless, you can achieve some level of success if you move beyond just identifying vacancies. If you learn there are no vacancies at present, push on to find out about application procedures. Many organizations maintain resume banks which they refer to when vacancies arise. If the company accepts resumes or applications, try to get the name of the person you should contact. In this case, the caller was able to get the name of two people. When she submits her resume to Mr. Merit, she can mention in her letter how helpful Mr. Plant was and that he recommended that she submit her resume for consideration. She now has two contacts and a resume in this organization. Not bad for what was probably a two minute call. If you make 100 such calls in a day, you should be able to collect 100 new names and submit 50 or more resumes.

RESPONDING TO ADS AND VACANCY ANNOUNCEMENTS

Most classified ads or vacancy announcement outline application procedures. Some may specifically state *"No phone calls please."* But the majority of employers will answer phone calls. Some may even encourage such calls because it indicates an interest in the position and company. At the same time, many applicants will call before they submit a resume and other documents for application. You are well advised to immediately call the company and ask for more information about the position. Read the ad carefully and list the questions you need addressed. You want to gather as much information about both the company and the position so you can "custom design" your resume and letter around the needs of the employer. Your call might go something like this:

CALLER: *"Hi, this is Beverly Rodriguez calling. Your ad in today's Post for a dental assistant caught my attention. I'm thinking about applying, but I need more information. Could you tell me a little more about the position and The Cooper Group?"*

RECEIVER: Responds to question with more information.

CALLER: *"That sounds interesting. You must work for a very exciting organization. I'll definitely submit my application. To whom should I address my resume?"*

RECEIVER: *"Send it to the attention of Tara Marks. She's in charge of handling this position."*

CALLER: *"By the way, do you know when she expects to make the final decision?"*

ANALYSIS: By calling for more information about the position and organization, the caller may gain some useful "inside" information that will give him an advantage over the competition. For example, she might learn that it's a 30-hour a week position with no benefits. She might work with five doctors rather than one. The company may be seeking someone with at least five years of experience. The job might involve traveling to several nursing homes. She might learn about the salary range. In addition, she may get the name of the person handling the screening process and thus better personalize her correspondence. When it comes time to follow-up, she has the name of the person to contact and knows when to best call. Needless to say, this phone call may yield some very valuable information that will help you both screen the employer and better develop an employer-centered application.

CLOSINGS

Similar to closing a job search letter, your telephone closing should end in some sort of future action. If you are closing a networking call, you should close with (1) an expression of gratitude, (2) a summary and interpretation of your conversation, and (3) a request for referrals. Your closing might go something like this:

CALLER: (EXPRESS GRATITUDE) *"I really appreciate the information you've given me on marketing opportunities in Eastern Europe and Russia.* (SUMMARIZE AND INTER-PRET PREVIOUS CONVERSATION) *You've identified five pharmaceutical companies that seem to have established a strong presence in at least five of these countries. If I understand you correctly, you feel there may be some excellent opportunities with these companies for someone with my interests and skills. I'm especially encouraged by your observation that some of these companies do have entry-level marketing positions overseas.* (REQUEST FOR REFERRALS) *Could I ask one more favor? Do you know two or three other people in this field who would be willing to talk to me about such marketing opportunities?"*

RECEIVER: *"You're quite welcome. Let me think. Yes, why don't you give Mary Sellers at Vialoriate International a call. Her number is 281-0091. John Baird at Southern Pharmaceuticals also would be a good person to contact. His number is 281-1121. It's okay to use my name. I've known them for years. Really good people who know this area well. Tell them I recommended you call them."*

CALLER: *"Thanks so much. Please keep me in mind if you hear of any opportunities for someone with my interests. Would it be okay to send you a copy of my resume for your reference?"*

RECEIVER: *"Sure. I'd be happy to keep it on file and pass it along if I hear of any opportunities."*

CALLER: *"Thanks again. Goodbye."*

ANALYSIS: This is the perfect closing. The job seeker actually managed to turn the closing into two, hopefully three, important actions: (1) received two referrals, (2) got the receiver to accept and read a resume for reference, and (3) requested to be remembered for future referrals which may indeed turn into new job contacts. However, one word of caution. This closing is not complete until it is followed up with a thank you letter which includes a copy of the resume and a request for future referrals. The thank you letter should genuinely express your gratitude for the person's time and information. For examples of such thank you letters, see our new edition of *Job Search Letters That Get Results: 201 Great Examples* (Impact Publications, 1995).

SCREENING INTERVIEW

The first job interview you will encounter is most likely to be a telephone screening interview. It might go something like this:

CALLER: *"Hi, this is Margo Zeller with Freedom Enterprises. We received your letter and resume of March 3rd in response to our ad for a production manager. You have a very interesting background that caught our attention. I have a few questions. Do you have a moment?"*

RECEIVER: *"Yes. How can I help you?"*

CALLER: *"You say in your resume that you received nine months of training in special production techniques. Can you elaborate on the nature of that training and where you received it?"*

RECEIVER: *"Sure. During the past five years I . . . ."*

CALLER: *"I notice you have an employment gap between 1985 and 1986. Is there some reason for this?"*

RECEIVER: *"Yes. During that time I was working on my Master's degree in production management. Those dates should appear under the education section for Louisiana State University."*

CALLER: *"What is your current employment situation in regards to availability?"*

RECEIVER: *"It's really flexible, depending on the nature of the offer. I'm obligated to give a two-week notice to my present employer. My family, of course, would be involved in any decision to relocate. It really depends on the situation."*

CALLER: *"This position requires some travel and weekend work. Would this present any problems for you?"*

RECEIVER: *"Not really. I'm used to traveling and putting in extra hours at work, including weekends."*

CALLER: *"What are your salary requirements?"*

RECEIVER: *"It depends on the position and responsibilities. I would need more information before I could give you a specific figure. What figure do you have in mind for someone with my qualifications?"*

CALLER: *"If we invited you to an interview, would you be available within the next week to fly to Seattle to meet with us?"*

RECEIVER: *"Right now I'd say yes. I would have to check my schedule and request leave time for such a visit. I don't see a problem."*

ANALYSIS: A screening interview is designed to both screen you in and screen you out of further consideration. In this scenario the interviewer asks a series of questions that could immediately disqualify the candidate if the answers appear too negative. The candidate tends to be either positive or open to further discussion. The salary question is one that must be handled delicately in a telephone screening interview. When the question arrives at this early stage in the interview process, it's best to keep it open by not stating a figure. Instead, turn the question around, as we've done in the case, and ask the interviewer to reveal his or her salary figure or range. By doing this, you may gain valuable salary information as well as keep yourself in the running by not disqualifying yourself so early in the interview game.

ANSWERING MACHINE
OR VOICE MAIL MESSAGE

Nothing is more irritating than to waste people's time with a lengthy voice mail message. Nothing will kill your chances of getting a job quicker than to have an important caller hear an unprofessional or silly message on your answering machine. Keep your answering machine or voice mail message simple, professional, and to the point. This one works well:

"Sorry I missed your call. Please leave your name, telephone number, and a message at the sound of the beep. I'll return your call as soon as possible. Thanks for calling."

FAX COVER PAGE

You may occasionally be asked to send faxes to prospective employ-ers. They may request a copy of your resume, samples of your writing, or other documents to support your candidacy. The most common fax request will be for a copy of your resume. When this happens, be sure to include a cover sheet which should also function as your cover letter for the resume. For example,

BRIAN TAYLOR
3218 West Front Street ▪ West Chester, PA 11911
Tel. 811-321-8111 ▪ Fax 811-321-8112

October 3, 1995

Wilson Olney
OLNEY GRAPHICS
832 Thomas Avenue
Chicago, IL 60000

Dear Mr. Olney:

The Graphic Artist position you advertised in today's <u>Chicago Tribune</u> fits me perfectly. I have the necessary motivation, skills, and experience to excel in this position.

As requested in your ad, I'm faxing you a copy of my resume. I have a strong background in computerized graphic design. As indicated in your ad, you need someone who has expertise with Microsoft, Excel, and Pagemaker and who can do layout and paste up. I've worked with all of these programs and do layout and paste up on a daily basis.

I'll call you Wednesday morning to see if we might get together soon to discuss this position. I'm interested in learning more about your studio.

Sincerely,

Brian Taylor

Brian Taylor

INDEX

THE
AUTHORS

Ronald L. Krannich, Ph.D. and **Caryl Rae Krannich, Ph.D.** operate Development Concepts Inc., a training, consulting, and publishing firm. Ron received his Ph.D. in Political Science from Northern Illinois University. Caryl received her Ph.D. in Speech Communication from Penn State University.

Caryl and Ron are former university professors, high school teachers, management trainers, and consultants. They have completed numerous projects on management, career development, local government, population planning, and rural development during the past twenty years. They have published several articles in major professional journals.

In addition to their extensive public sector work, the Krannichs are two of America's leading career and travel writers. They are authors of 31 career books and 11 travel books. Their career books focus on key job search skills, government jobs, international careers, nonprofit organizations, and career transitions. Their work represents one of today's most extensive and highly praised collections of career writing with such bestsellers as *The Almanac of International Jobs and Careers, Best Jobs for the 1990s and Into the 21st Century, Change Your Job Change Your Life, Dynamite Answers to Interview Questions, Dynamite Cover Letters, Dynamite Resumes, Find a Federal Job Fast, From Army Green to Corporate Gray, High Impact Resumes and Letters, Interview for Success, Job Search Letters That Get Results, Jobs for People Who Love Travel,* and *The New Network Your Way to Job and Career Success.* Their books are found in most major bookstores, libraries, and career centers. Many of their works are now available interactively on CD-ROM (*Job-Power Source*).

Ron and Caryl continue to pursue their international interests through their innovative *Treasures and Pleasures of Exotic Places* travel series. When they are not found at their home and business in Virginia, they are probably somewhere in Hong Kong, China, Thailand, Malaysia, Singapore, Indonesia, Papua New Guinea, Australia, New Zealand, Tahiti, Fiji, Burma, India, Nepal, Morocco, Turkey, Mexico, Italy, or the Caribbean pursuing their other passion—shopping and traveling for quality arts and antiques.

CAREER RESOURCES

*C*ontact Impact Publications to receive a free copy of their latest comprehensive and annotated catalog of career resources (hundreds of books, directories, subscriptions, training programs, audiocassettes, videos, computer software programs, multimedia, and CD-ROM).

The following career resources, many of which are mentioned in previous chapters, are available directly from Impact Publications. Complete the following form or list the titles, include shipping (see formula at the end), enclose payment, and send your order to:

IMPACT PUBLICATIONS
9104-N Manassas Drive
Manassas Park, VA 22111-5211
Tel. 703/361-7300
Fax 703/335-9486

Orders from individuals must be prepaid by check, moneyorder, Visa or MasterCard number. We accept telephone and fax orders with a Visa or MasterCard number.

Qty.	TITLES	Price	TOTAL
JOB SEARCH STRATEGIES AND TACTICS			
___	Change Your Job, Change Your Life	$15.95	___
___	Complete Job Finder's Guide to the 90's	$13.95	___
___	Dynamite Tele-Search	$12.95	___
___	Five Secrets to Finding a Job	$12.95	___
___	How to Get Interviews From Classified Job Ads	$14.95	___
___	How to Succeed Without a Career Path	$13.95	___
___	Job-Power Source CD-ROM	$49.95	___
___	Rites of Passage at $100,000+	$29.95	___
___	What Color Is Your Parachute?	$14.95	___

129

TELEPHONE AND JOB HOTLINE DIRECTORIES

___ Directory of Executive Recruiters $39.95   _____
___ Encyclopedia of Associations $990.00   _____
___ Government Directory of Addresses
    and Telephone Numbers $149.95   _____
___ Job Hotlines USA $24.95   _____
___ Job Hunter's Yellow Pages $59.00   _____
___ National Directory of Addresses and
    Telephone Numbers $99.95   _____

JOB VACANCY SOURCEBOOKS

___ Government Job Finder $16.95   _____
___ Non-Profit's Job Finder $16.95   _____
___ Professional's Private Sector Job Finder $18.95   _____

ELECTRONIC JOB SEARCH RESOURCES

___ Electronic Job Search Revolution $12.95   _____
___ Electronic Resume Revolution $12.95   _____
___ Electronic Resumes for the New Job Market $11.95   _____
___ Hook Up, Get Hired $12.95   _____
___ On-Line Job Search Companion $14.95   _____
___ Using the Internet in Your Job Search $16.95   _____

BEST JOBS AND EMPLOYERS FOR THE 90's

___ 100 Best Companies to Work for in America $27.95   _____
___ Adams Jobs Almanac 1995 $12.95   _____
___ American Almanac of Jobs and Salaries $17.00   _____
___ Best Jobs for the 1990s and Into the 21st Century $19.95   _____
___ Hoover's Guide to Computer Companies (with disk) $34.95   _____
___ Hoover's Masterlist of 2,500 of America's
    Largest and Fastest Growing Employers (with disk) $19.95   _____
___ Job Seeker's Guide to 1000 Top Employers $22.95   _____
___ Jobs 1995 $15.00   _____

KEY DIRECTORIES

___ American Almanac of Jobs and Salaries $17.00   _____
___ American Salaries and Wages Survey $99.95   _____
___ Career Training Sourcebook $24.95   _____
___ Careers Encyclopedia $39.95   _____
___ Dictionary of Occupational Titles $39.95   _____
___ Encyclopedia of Careers & Vocational Guidance $129.95   _____
___ Hoover's American Business $29.95   _____
___ Hoover's World Business $27.95   _____
___ Job Bank Guide to Employment Services $149.95   _____
___ Job Hunter's Sourcebook $69.95   _____
___ Moving and Relocation Directory $179.95   _____
___ National Fax Directory $89.00   _____
___ National Job Bank $249.95   _____
___ National Trade and Professional Associations $79.95   _____
___ Occupational Outlook Handbook $21.95   _____

___ Personnel Executives Contactbook $149.00 _____
___ Professional Careers Sourcebook $89.95 _____
___ Vocational Careers Sourcebook $79.95 _____

CITY AND STATE JOB FINDERS (Adams Media's Job Banks)

___ Atlanta $15.95 _____
___ Boston $15.95 _____
___ Chicago $15.95 _____
___ Dallas/Fort Worth $15.95 _____
___ Denver $15.95 _____
___ Florida $15.95 _____
___ Houston $15.95 _____
___ Los Angeles $15.95 _____
___ Minneapolis $15.95 _____
___ New York $15.95 _____
___ Philadelphia $15.95 _____
___ San Francisco $15.95 _____
___ Seattle $15.95 _____
___ Washington, DC $15.95 _____

CITY AND STATE JOB FINDERS (Surrey Books)

___ Atlanta $15.95 _____
___ Boston $15.95 _____
___ Dallas/Fort Worth $15.95 _____
___ Houston $15.95 _____
___ New York $15.95 _____
___ San Francisco $15.95 _____
___ Seattle and Portland $15.95 _____
___ Southern California $15.95 _____
___ Washington, DC $15.95 _____

ALTERNATIVE JOBS AND CAREERS

___ Advertising Career Directory $17.95 _____
___ Business and Finance Career Directory $17.95 _____
___ But What If I Don't Want to Go to College? $10.95 _____
___ Career Opportunities in the Sports Industry $27.95 _____
___ Careers in Accounting $16.95 _____
___ Careers in Communications $16.95 _____
___ Careers in Computers $16.95 _____
___ Careers in Engineering $16.95 _____
___ Careers in Health Care $16.95 _____
___ Careers in High Tech $16.95 _____
___ Environmental Career Directory $17.95 _____
___ Marketing and Sales Career Directory $17.95 _____
___ Outdoor Careers $14.95 _____
___ Radio and Television Career Directory $17.95 _____
___ Travel and Hospitality Career Directory $17.95 _____

INTERNATIONAL, OVERSEAS, AND TRAVEL JOBS

___ Almanac of International Jobs and Careers $19.95 _____
___ Complete Guide to International Jobs & Careers $13.95 _____

___ Guide to Careers in World Affairs $14.95 ___
___ How to Get a Job in Europe $17.95 ___
___ Jobs for People Who Love Travel $15.95 ___
___ Jobs in Russia and the Newly Independent States $15.95 ___

PUBLIC-ORIENTED CAREERS

___ Almanac of American Government Jobs and Careers $14.95 ___
___ Complete Guide to Public Employment $19.95 ___
___ Directory of Federal Jobs and Employers $21.95 ___
___ Federal Applications That Get Results $23.95 ___
___ Federal Jobs in Law Enforcement $15.95 ___
___ Find a Federal Job Fast! $12.95 ___
___ Government Job Finder $16.95 ___
___ Jobs and Careers With Nonprofit Organizations $15.95 ___

JOB LISTINGS & VACANCY ANNOUNCEMENTS

___ Executive Recruiter News $157.00 ___
___ Federal Career Opportunities (6 biweekly issues) $39.00 ___
___ International Employment Gazette (6 biweekly issues) $35.00 ___

SKILLS, TESTING, SELF-ASSESSMENT

___ Discover the Best Jobs for You $11.95 ___
___ Do What You Are $15.95 ___
___ Do What You Love, the Money Will Follow $11.95 ___
___ I Could Do Anything If I Only Know What It Was $19.95 ___
___ Where Do I Go With the Rest of My Life? $11.95 ___
___ Wishcraft $14.95 ___

RESUMES, LETTERS, & NETWORKING

___ Dynamite Cover Letters $11.95 ___
___ Dynamite Resumes $11.95 ___
___ Electronic Resumes for the New Job Market $11.95 ___
___ Great Connections $11.95 ___
___ High Impact Resumes and Letters $14.95 ___
___ How to Work a Room $9.95 ___
___ Job Search Letters That Get Results $15.95 ___
___ New Network Your Way to Job and Career Success $15.95 ___

DRESS, APPEARANCE, IMAGE

___ 110 Mistakes Working Women Make/Dressing Smart $9.95 ___
___ John Molloy's New Dress for Success $10.95 ___
___ Red Socks Don't Work! (Men's Clothing) $14.95 ___

INTERVIEWS & SALARY NEGOTIATIONS

___ 60 Seconds and You're Hired! $9.95 ___
___ Dynamite Answers to Interview Questions $11.95 ___
___ Dynamite Salary Negotiation $12.95 ___
___ Interview for Success $13.95 ___
___ Sweaty Palms $9.95 ___

MILITARY

___ From Air Force Blue to Corporate Gray $17.95 _____
___ From Army Green to Corporate Gray $15.95 _____
___ From Navy Blue to Corporate Gray $17.95 _____
___ Job Search: Marketing Your Military Experience $14.95 _____
___ Resumes and Cover Letters for
Transitioning Military Personnel $17.95

WOMEN AND SPOUSES

___ Doing It All Isn't Everything $19.95 _____
___ New Relocating Spouse's Guide to Employment $14.95 _____
___ Resumes for Re-Entry: A Handbook for Women $10.95 _____
___ Survival Guide for Women $16.95 _____

MINORITIES AND DISABLED

___ Best Companies for Minorities $12.00
___ Directory of Special Programs for
Minority Group Members $31.95 _____
___ Job Strategies for People With Disabilities $14.95 _____
___ Minority Organizations $49.95 _____
___ Work, Sister, Work $19.95 _____

ENTREPRENEURSHIP AND SELF-EMPLOYMENT

___ 101 Best Businesses to Start $15.00
___ Best Home-Based Businesses for the 90s $11.95 _____
___ Entrepreneur's Guide to Starting a Successful Business $16.95 _____
___ Have You Got What It Takes? $12.95 _____

VIDEOS

___ Dialing for Jobs $139.00
___ Directing Your Successful Job Search $99.95 _____
___ Find the Job You Want...and Get It! $229.95 _____
___ Looking Ahead $129.95 _____
___ Winning At Job Hunting in the 90s $89.95 _____

COMPUTER SOFTWARE PROGRAMS (IBM or Compatibles)

___ Cambridge Career Counseling System $349.00
___ INSTANT Job Hunting Letters $39.95 _____
___ JobHunt for Window® $59.95 _____
___ Resumemaker With Career Planning $49.95 _____
___ WinWay Resume and Interviewing $69.95 _____
___ You're Hired! $59.95 _____

CD-ROM

___ America's Top Jobs $295.00
___ CD-ROM Version of the Occupational
Outlook Handbook $399.00 _____

___ Electronic Guide for Occupational Exploration	$295.00	___
___ Encyclopedia of Careers and Vocational Guidance	$199.95	___
___ Interview Skills of the Future	$199.00	___
___ Job-Power Source (Individual Version)	$49.95	___
___ Job-Power Source (Professional Version with DOT)	$149.95	___
___ Job Search Skills of the 21st Century	$199.00	___
___ Multimedia Career Center	$385.00	___
___ National Directory of Addresses and Telephone Numbers	$150.00	___
___ Occupational Outlook On CD-ROM	$29.95	___
___ Resume Revolution	$99.00	___
___ Tech Prep Careers for the Future	$349.00	___

SUBTOTAL   _____

Virginia residents add 4½% sales tax   _____

POSTAGE/HANDLING ($4 for first
product and $1 for each additional) $4.00

Number of additional titles x $1.00 ---------- _____

TOTAL ENCLOSED ----------------- _____

NAME _____

ADDRESS _____

_____

_____

❐   I enclose check/moneyorder for $ _____ made
     payable to IMPACT PUBLICATIONS.

❐   Please charge $ _____ to my credit card:

     Card # _____

     Expiration date: _____ / _____

     Signature _____

SEND TO: IMPACT PUBLICATIONS, 9104-N Manassas Drive, Manassas Park,
            VA 22111-5211, Tel. 703/361-7300 or Fax 703/335-9486